SAILING TOWARD HORIZON
A LEADERSHIP VOYAGE OF DISCOVERY

Sailing Toward
HORIZON

— A LEADERSHIP VOYAGE OF DISCOVERY —

GARY WHITELEY

LUMINARE PRESS

WWW.LUMINAREPRESS.COM

Sailing Toward Horizon: A Leadership Voyage of Discovery
Copyright © 2023 by Gary Whiteley

All rights reserved. This book or any portion thereof may not be reproduced or used in any manner whatsoever without the express written permission of the publisher, except for the use of brief quotations in a book review.

Printed in the United States of America

Luminare Press
442 Charnelton St.
Eugene, OR 97401
www.luminarepress.com

LCCN: 2023907315
ISBN: 979-8-88679-165-5

This book is dedicated to Bob Garmston, Art Costa, and Gordy Donaldson for their wisdom and inspiration.

Table of Contents

Foreword ix
Preface xiii
Acknowledgments xix
Introduction xxiii

The CANAM Smart Ports and Harbors Program 1

DAY ONE—Introduction and Communicating to Understand and to Influence, from Mosquito Creek Marina-North Vancouver via Nanaimo to Ladysmith 11

DAY TWO—Interdependent Thinking and Acting, from Ladysmith to Sidney 41

DAY THREE—Gathering Information for Improvement and Innovation, Sidney to Friday Harbor 56

DAY FOUR—Seeking Support and Feedback that Fosters Growth, Friday Harbor to La Conner Harbor 71

DAY FIVE—Adaptive Competence, from La Conner Harbor to Mosquito Creek Marina 87

The CAGIS Foundation Team Debrief 106

Appendix A Communicating to Understand and to Influence . . 119
Appendix B Interdependent Thinking and Acting 122
Appendix C Adaptive Competence 125
Endnotes 128
Index 132
About the Author 145

Foreword

It might seem unusual that a school superintendent would be on the front line of addressing the consequences of climate change. I never imagined that as the leader of the Lower Kuskokwim School District located in Western Alaska, I would be confronted with relocating schools and assisting communities in relocating essential infrastructure due to rising sea levels, riverbank erosion, thawing permafrost, and catastrophic weather events such as Typhoon Merbok in September 2022.

The challenge of relocating a community and its school is a complex endeavor that involves federal agencies, state and local governmental organizations, city governments, sovereign tribal governments, and the school board. A complicating factor for the Lower Kuskokwim School District is the responsibility of generating primary electrical power for two villages, providing water in thirteen villages, and wastewater treatment for five villages. It is an enormous challenge to maintain and support the infrastructure for twenty-nine schools across approximately 22,000 square miles with few roads, unforgiving Alaskan winter weather, and ever-increasing severe weather events.

The bipartisan federal infrastructure law allocated $50 million to relocate two villages in our region. The State of Alaska has approved $25 million, and an additional $56 million is anticipated to demolish and relocate one school in the Lower Kuskokwim School District. It is conceivable that eight to ten villages and schools in our region will need to be relocated within the next decade. I have provided this background information to illustrate the complexities involved in addressing the consequences of climate change and the incredible need for thoughtful and skillful leadership. The solutions for relocating remote villages and their community schools are neither simple nor self-evident. The ongoing process of adapting as individuals and communities is not a straightforward path. I have witnessed solution-minded strategies emerge from community conversations, as well as the predictable human emotions of frustration, fear, and anger. I have relied heavily on many of the practices and strategies in *Sailing Toward Horizon: A Leadership Voyage of Discovery*.

I have struggled at times when emotions are intense, some people have been verbally aggressive and made hurtful comments, and my human inclination is to become defensive or to attempt to avoid conflict altogether. There is a treasure trove of practices and strategies in the chapter "Communicating to Understand and to Influence" that provides structures for more productive and organized group interactions. Developing personal presence, listening with empathy, and learning to paraphrase accurately have been essential for a productive community dialogue.

The process of engaging communities about relocating their homes, essential infrastructure, and schools has been more difficult because of the Covid-19 pandemic. Many villages in the Lower Kuskokwim School District placed strict Covid-19 travel and quarantine restrictions within their communities because of memories aroused by the tragic consequences of the 1918–19 Spanish Flu epidemic, which had a devastating impact on Alaska Native communities. The "Iñupiat village of Brevig Mission, Alaska, where 72 of the 80 Iñupiat residents died of influenza within five days" occurred in November 1918.[1] Many villages in the Lower Kuskokwim School District reported similar devastation. The consequences of climate change can only be addressed with a keen understanding of a cultural context and all the concern, emotion, and ambiguity of a clear path forward that accompanies it. The challenges of addressing climate change are intertwined with the past, the present, and an uncertain future.

The technique of creating an experience aboard a boat on a

voyage of discovery creates an opportunity to step away from daily activities and reflect on what might be possible as a leader and a team member. A major theme in Gary's book is that it requires a team of committed individuals to address complex challenges. "I alone can fix it" is a leadership strategy that is bound to fail when so many challenges emerge simultaneously. The use of fictional characters is an intriguing way to introduce leadership skills, and I identify with aspects of all five characters in the book.

Marit-Abriel Hanson's reserved demeanor and strong resolve are two characteristics I am especially drawn toward. I have two young children, and my hope is that I can model these characteristics in both personal and professional settings. I appreciate and feel acquainted with Lincoln Angiak, the book character and tugboat captain from Quinhagak. I was once a young teacher in Quinhagak, and it is a village that is threatened by melting permafrost, a rising sea level, and riverbank erosion. It is also a village with a school in the Lower Kuskokwim School District.

I welcome you to the front line of climate change. We can read the scientific reports and the predictions they posit about how much sequestered methane will be released by thawing tundra, how much warmer the atmospheric temperature of earth will become, how much higher the sea level will rise, and how much more severe weather events will become. Meanwhile, for those of us addressing the consequences of a warming planet on an hourly basis, we need frameworks and resources for *collaborating with* individuals, agencies, and communities.

I encourage you to add *Sailing Toward Horizon: A Leadership Voyage of Discovery* as a primary resource and consider it a leadership survival guide for working on the front lines of the unpredictable and at times devastating impact of global climate change.

Kimberly Hankins
Superintendent of Schools, Lower Kuskokwim School District
February 2023

Preface

The ideas and themes in *Sailing Toward Horizon: A Leadership Voyage of Discovery* have occupied my thinking for fifteen years. I started authoring an unnamed book in 2015 that was nautical by nature—meaning the main characters were mariners, and a leadership voyage would take place aboard an oceangoing vessel. The book would include people from diverse ethnic backgrounds, nationalities, and religious affiliations and would hopefully appeal to a wide audience. It was an exploration and examination of my own beliefs about how potential leaders might acquire the knowledge and wisdom to create a path forward through the unprecedented challenges of climate change.

If the challenges of climate change are to be addressed, it will require that all hands must be on deck. *Sailing Toward Horizon: A Leadership Voyage of Discovery* presents a leadership framework that is an alternative to the Great Man leadership style. This traditional Great Man leadership style is incapable of addressing and partly responsible for the magnitude of the challenges of rising sea levels and ocean acidification that cause *climigration*—forced migration due to climate change. The characters within the book needed to be diverse, to have authentic formative life experiences, and to be willing to seek guidance from *wisdom keepers*, as Barry Lopez, the celebrated author and National Book Award winner, often described leaders within traditional communities.

Wisdom keepers are individuals who emerge with the interest and health of their respective communities as a primary focus when confronted with an uncertain future. In other words, one might ask: Who is on the bridge of the ship, and where might they lead us? I finally summoned the courage to write Barry Lopez in late August 2020 and described the focus of the book I was writing. The Holiday Farm Fire, in the western Cascade Mountains of Oregon, destroyed his sacred home, outbuildings, and surrounding forest on the McKenzie River in early September. I received a heartfelt and thoughtful reply from Barry created on an IBM typewriter in mid-November, about five weeks before "he could cross his river now," as his beloved wife, Debra, described his passing on Christmas Day. It was an emotional experience to know that Barry took the time to write as his health and life were fading.

I was crestfallen to learn the news of Barry's passing. I cannot say we were friends. I can say that I have resided in Alaska since 1975 and read many of his books and articles that were inspired by his trips to Alaska and the Canadian Arctic. His work spoke to me, and it felt as though we were brothers in spirit since I first read Barry's work in the mid-1980s. It would have been the honor of a lifetime to call him a friend. Debra, Barry's wife, noted on barrylopez.com that he would often say, "I want to live a life that helped." I assert that Barry also lived a life that inspired others to think clearly and deeply about the natural world and our role within it and to act toward shaping a better tomorrow. It is my humble hope that *Sailing Toward Horizon: A Leadership Voyage of Discovery*, a title inspired by Barry's amazing life, might illuminate a path toward shaping a better future.

Sailing Toward Horizon: A Leadership Voyage of Discovery asserts that leadership opportunities for people from different continents and cultures must be available to address the causes and consequences of climate change. Historically, the Great Man has been the dominant archetype in most organizations. Any leader-centric model that focuses on one person being in charge is inadequate when communities, nongovernmental organizations, nonprofit foundations, for-profit businesses, and social entrepreneurs need to cooperate and collaborate to craft solutions to complex problems from the impact and effects of global warming. The Great Man archetype, and many variants, are deeply embedded in our leadership DNA. It is the default position for many contemporary leaders and has been well-documented in the business and military leadership literature for well over one hundred years.

The Great Man archetype was well-aligned with the Industrial Age. Management for industrial mass production was a predictable, rule-based system organized around a bureaucratic hierarchy with information controlled by a few men at the top. The Great Man archetype is grounded in the belief that true leaders are born with intrinsic traits, elitist because of birthright and education, and not accessible to most people because of their station in life. It is a leadership model that aligns perfectly with industrial-age mass production. Many business organizations easily divorced ethical decision-making from company goals and profit margins, which in some cases resulted in catastrophic environmental consequences. These business organizations made their decisions unaware and unconcerned about how socially and economically vulnerable people were, and still are, as they experienced the brunt of the effects of environmental degradation and global warming.

Sailing Toward Horizon: A Leadership Voyage of Discovery describes how *leadership can be modeled and learned, is dispositional by design, and is evidenced by demonstrating capabilities and practices.* Leadership is a *contingency activity,* meaning that leaders draw upon and utilize practices and behaviors as they *assess* a situation. Intelligent thinking by those in leadership roles must be multifaceted and include rational intelligence, emotional intelligence, social intelligence, and collective intelligence. Scientific knowledge and Traditional Ecological Knowledge (TEK) are both regarded equally without judging or discounting the value each might bring to our understanding.

It is possible for leaders to focus on the greater good and the needs of their respective communities while being capable of setting aside their own self-interest. The capacity to serve and lead others is best told through narrative stories because personal character development and ethical decision-making are intertwined and inseparable from our professional selves. Case studies used by elite business schools, such as that of the 2010 Deepwater Horizon catastrophe that killed eleven and is regarded as the largest marine oil spill in history, carefully documented decision-making failures. US District Court Judge Barbier said that reckless gross negligence and willful misconduct described the conduct of the companies involved in this environmental disaster.

Sailing Toward Horizon: A Leadership Voyage of Discovery follows the development of leaders whose personal character and ethical qualities demonstrate that ethical conduct can be learned and *not* repeated by exploring an organization's failures and carefully analyzing the decision-making errors and timelines. The Deepwater Horizon oil rig was considered a marvel of sophisticated technology and managed by highly skilled leaders. The owners and operators ultimately relied upon a faulty moral compass, despite deploying amazing technology and attracting highly capable managers. In this book, you will explore how the foundation for an ethic of concern is built by the experiences of the main characters, who understand that we all benefit when we have empathy and concern for others and for the physical world around us.

The hierarchical superordinate/subordinate relationship is a hallmark of the Great Man paradigm, a professional hierarchical relationship that is *not* based upon the behaviors of listening, understanding, empathizing, or acknowledging that all members of a group have equal status. Barry Lopez, in his published work and during interviews, characterized these behaviors as uniquely human behaviors and a possible starting point for addressing global climate change. If these behaviors were *default positions* when humans first encounter or interact with one another, then environmental degradation would be anomalies and not the all too predictable occurrences that are reported around the globe. We must consider incorporating these uniquely human capabilities into addressing the complex problems that challenge our very existence as a species. We will need to draw upon the best qualities of our common humanity, adapt our behavior, and rely less upon an ever-increasing expectation that technology alone will solve the challenges we face.

Conventional wisdom suggests that the world is cold and indifferent; the strong will dominate, the weak will perish, and the powerful will assert their will. Leaders compete and conquer rivals in a zero-sum game: for me to win, you must lose. We observe daily the absolute failure of leadership by individuals and organizations motivated by self-interest and greed-based transactional relationships. It is unsurprising that so many people are cynical and have little faith in our institutions or hope that significant challenges can be addressed. Does it really need to be this way? Can leadership be capable of inspiring others to address complex problems? Can we develop a better and more peaceful world?

Sailing Toward Horizon: A Leadership Voyage of Discovery is literally a voyage that takes place on water. The fictional characters are developed through life experiences and formal education. The book provides a rationale for why leadership needs to be different, as well as a guide with many examples of how to support leadership within a team or group. Leadership development should be inclusive and accessible to anyone open to learning and willing to incorporate new ways of thinking and doing in a supportive and collegial environment. Do these notions sound like unrealistic expectations, a bridge too far, wishful thinking for the naïve and uninitiated? I hope not. The challenges of addressing climate change will require an unprecedented level of collaboration and trust between individuals and organizations. I share both a quality and a concern voiced by Barry Lopez. The quality: I am an optimist. The concern: time is running out to proactively respond to the impact of global warming.

Gary Whiteley
Kenai, Alaska
June 2023

Acknowledgments

I would like to thank those colleagues who were instrumental in my growth and understanding of leadership and learning. The wonderful cadre of professors at the University of Maine, Gordon Donaldson, Russ Quaglia, Dean Robert "Bob" Cobb, Walter McIntire, Jonathan Plucker, and Ted Coladarci. It is always a gift to be intellectually stimulated and supported by educators who are brilliant.

The former leaders at the Alaska Department of Education and Early Development, Commissioner Roger Sampson, Deputy Commissioner Les Morse, and Deputy Commissioner Barbara Thompson made it possible through the Alaska Administrator Coaching Project to provide learning opportunities and mentoring for six hundred school principals from 2004 through 2015. They are owed a debt of gratitude for securing funding and for their visionary leadership. The mentors who collaborated with the Alaskan principals, Carol Kane, Jim Gillis, Tom Briscoe, Dave Cloud, Sandra Lanning, Sandra Hill, Reed Carlson, Randy Swenson, Mick Wykis, and Larry Nauta traveled for school visits via small aircraft, boats, and snow machines to the remote areas of Alaska. The mentors were an amazing group of resolute educators who frequently slept on wrestling mats in school gymnasiums and ate cold food while waiting for a small plane delayed by inclement weather. As a team we helped school leaders implement the material in the book *Dispositions of Leadership: The Effects on Student Learning and School Culture*.[2]

Our collective experiences formed the basis for *Sailing Toward Horizon: A Leadership Voyage of Discovery*. (The effects of climate change were ever present during our trips to remote Alaska.)

Former Idaho Superintendent of Public Instruction Sherri Ybarra and School Improvement Coordinator Tyson Carter made it possible to work with over 300 school leaders throughout Idaho from 2011 through 2020. Thank you. The mentors who collaborated with principals in Idaho were Patti Odell, Jeff Read, Wiley Dobbs, Alice Hocklander, Sue Beitia, and Nancy Chopko. They are remarkable people. The mentors in Alaska and Idaho, and many of the principals in both leadership programs, were never shy about providing valuable feedback about what materials seemed to work, what needed revision, and what needed to be retired. Thank you!

Shelby Skaanes, Lexie Domaradzki, Bobbi Jo Erb, and Mick Wykis are four amazing consultants and colleagues. I owe them a debt of gratitude. They have taught me wonderful techniques for working with adults. The current and former leaders in Lower Kuskokwim School District (LKSD) I have worked alongside for fifteen years inspired me to continue addressing the effects of climate change. Thank you to former Superintendent Daniel Walker and former Assistant Superintendent Carlton Kuhns who made it possible to work in a school district that is about 22,000 square miles with few roads. (LKSD is about the size of West Virginia.) LKSD Superintendent Kimberly Hankins and Assistant Superintendent Edward Pekar are amazing educators, colleagues, and friends. They are addressing the aftermath of Typhoon Merbok, which devastated the western coast of Alaska in September 2022. (More evidence that we need significant human and financial resources to address rising sea levels and community shattering weather events.)

Robert J. Garmston and Arthur L. Costa's influence is present on many pages of this book. Their knowledge about thinking dispositions, coaching adults, and working with groups is remarkable. This book would not have been possible without their insights and wisdom. I thank Patty Muller, Christopher Frisella, and Sallie

McCann Vandagrift for their editing expertise.

Mary, my wife and partner for 48 years, designed this book's cover and map. I owe her a double debt of gratitude for the artwork and her support.

Introduction

Sailing Toward Horizon: A Leadership Voyage of Discovery is a fictionalized biography. The creation of composite fictional characters enhances an author's ability to develop a story that is, hopefully, compelling. The five main characters are a diverse group of individuals who develop into a supportive and dynamic team. Marit-Abril Hansen's father is from Alaska, of Norwegian descent, and her mother is from Argentina. Jean-Philippe Gagnon has French Canadian roots from Quebec with family from Michigan. Nora Jensen is from Belgium. Lincoln Angiak is from the western Arctic coast of Alaska. Erika Knudsen's father is from Denmark, and her mother is from Thailand. She resides with her partner, Monique, in the Faroe Islands, the Kingdom of Denmark.

Marit-Abril, Jean-Philippe, Nora, Lincoln, and Erika share an ethos of caring for the natural world, learned through their varied experiences and reinforced through constructive interactions with other human beings. Through telling the story of each main character, we see how their personal and professional lives are intricately intertwined in ways that are impossible to separate. *Sailing Toward Horizon: A Leadership Voyage of Discovery* takes place aboard the *RV Smart Ports*, a research vessel turned into a floating learning lab. As participants in the journey aboard a floating classroom, you are invited to learn while sailing on a very precious natural resource: water.

Water is a constant companion for the main characters, as it has been for humanity since before recorded history. Water makes up 50 percent to 75 percent of our bodies, depending on age and gender.[3] We can die if we do not drink enough or consume too much of it. Seventy percent of the earth's surface is covered by water. About 40 percent of the world's population lives within 100 kilometers of it. Approximately 90 percent of the world's economic trade is shipped on water.[4]

We recreate on water and in water. We drink, bathe, and grow crops using water. We harvest food from it and mine natural resources below it. At the same time, we pollute it, neglect it, and can no longer take it for granted. Due to indifference, ignorance, and neglect, our precious resource, water, is in trouble—and so are we. As water changes in massive quantities from a frozen state to a liquid form in the Antarctic and the Arctic, we will need to consider fleeing from it. As we consume enormous amounts of petroleum products and seek deposits of rare-earth metals, there is an aggressive competition between nations to see who claims the natural resources below the polar regions.

Sailing Toward Horizon: A Leadership Voyage of Discovery features a large, fictional international grant called the CANAM Smart Ports and Harbors Program. The grant is titled CANAM to acknowledge the unprecedented cooperation between the United States of America and Canada, two allies who share approximately 9,000 kilometers of unguarded international border, the longest in the world. These two allies are free and democratic nations that have enjoyed a mutually beneficial free trade relationship for decades—a relationship that has been needlessly strained in recent years. The CANAM Smart Ports and Harbors Program grant illustrates what mutual and respectful cooperation looks like and might accomplish.

The main characters in this book, Marit-Abril, Lincoln, Erika, Jean-Philippe, and Nora, join to form the CAGIS Foundation, based in North Vancouver, British Columbia. The CAGIS team teaches the *Dispositions of Leadership* to the CANAM Smart Ports and Harbors Program grant recipients. CAGIS is the first letter of the five dispositions: (1) *Communicating to Understand and to Influence*, (2) *Adaptive Competence*, (3) *Gathering Information for Improvement and Innovation*, (4) *Interdependent Thinking and Acting*, and (5) *Seeking Support and Feedback*.[5] The CAGIS *Dispositions of Leadership* framework is an innovative *default* leadership mindset for organizations addressing complex problems. These problems and challenges are often unpredictable and are addressed most effectively when information is transparent and shared openly. Potential solutions to these types of complex problems and challenges can only be implemented through extensive sustained cooperation and collaboration of many interested individuals and groups.

The CAGIS Foundation was formed around a global commitment to ensuring the dignity of every person by improving the quality of life for coastal communities. These chapters include the decision by Marit-Abril, Lincoln, Nora, and Jean-Philippe to broaden the team to include Dr. Ericka Knudsen, emeritus professor of leadership studies and cognitive science at the University of Copenhagen. Together Marit-Abril, Nora, Jean-Philippe, Lincoln, and Erika explore the rationale and guiding principles of the new charitable foundation, challenge their previous thinking about leadership, and develop the dispositions that form not only the core of the foundation but also its very name.

The CAGIS Foundation's first major project is a Five-Day Leadership Training at Sea. Four of the largest charitable foundations in the world announce grants totaling $446 million in US dollars to develop smart cities with smart ports in three locations: two in Canada and one in the United States. Coastal cities in the United States and Canada are invited to submit proposals for the CANAM Smart Ports and Harbors Program grant. The CAGIS Foundation's principal role in the program is to provide visionary leadership training for all participating organizations.

Marit-Abril, Lincoln, Nora, Erika, and Jean-Philippe decided that training in the five *Dispositions of Leadership* would provide a common mindset and a common language for the leaders of all organizations participating in the CANAM Smart Ports and Harbors Program grant. The CAGIS team believes that a five-day journey featuring one disposition each day aboard a floating classroom would assist all participants in forming strong bonds with each other. Their hope is by learning new capabilities and skills together, the entire team will address the effects of global warming that may elude the independent-minded unwilling to respond interdependently.

The five-day journey features each disposition in a corresponding location: (1) *Communicating to Understand and to Influence* starting in Vancouver; (2) *Interdependent Thinking and Acting* starting in Ladysmith, British Columbia; (3) *Gathering Information for Improvement and Innovation* starting in Sidney, British Columbia; (4) *Seeking Support and Feedback* in Friday Harbor, Washington; and (5) *Adaptive Competence* starting in La Conner Harbor, Washington. Chapters Two through Six provide the primary content and materials for each of the five days of the leadership training journey focused on the five leadership dispositions. The concluding chapter recounts Marit-Abril, Lincoln, Nora, Erika, and Jean-Philippe's debriefing after they return to port in North Vancouver, British Columbia, as well as provides Marit-Abril's thoughts about her future and her hopes for the future of the CAGIS Foundation.

As the reader, you will be asked to explore ideas in each chapter. The Questions to Engage Your Thinking at the end of each chapter will hopefully lead to your own leadership insights or thoughtful conversation with colleagues. Chapter Two (Communicating to Understand and to Influence), Chapter Three (Interdependent Thinking and Acting), and Chapter Six (Adaptive Competence) have an appendix for exploring how you might apply the information for these three dispositions in a team setting.

The setting for the book is on the water, a common liquid we take for granted, and aboard ships and boats that transport much of the material we need to exist. The capabilities and practices associated with each leadership disposition can be utilized even if you are a landlubber and not associated with an organization addressing climate change. Here are a few questions to get you thinking:

1. What concerns might you have about rising sea levels and melting polar ice? Why would you make a water environment the setting for a book about leadership?

It is asserted that a new *default leadership mindset* is needed for organizations and individuals wanting to solve complex problems requiring unprecedented cooperation and collaboration.

2. As a leader or in observing other leaders, what approaches, and dispositional thinking have been used in addressing complex problems? In what ways and to what degree were these approaches effective?

Chapter One

The CANAM Smart Ports and Harbors Program

A Program Establishing Smart Ports/Smart Harbors in Three Coastal Zones

The news arrived so quickly that Marit-Abril's initial response was a wave of apprehension. When the other team members read the letter, they were euphoric, followed by the realization that the commitments made in a grant application would need to happen sooner rather than later. Within six months of forming the CAGIS Foundation, the five-member team of Marit-Abril Hansen, Erika Knudsen, Nora Jensen, Lincoln Angiak, and Jean-Philippe Gagnon were informed they would be participating in a project funded by four of the largest charitable foundations in the world. The diverse team had formed solid professional relationships and strong personal bonds. Marit-Abril, Erika, Nora, Lincoln, and Jean-Philippe brought different strengths, a wealth of experiences, and divergent perspectives that made their deliberations intense, respectful, and productive. These qualities are why their response to CANAM Smart Ports and Harbors Program was successful.

The grant award to the CAGIS Foundation totaled $446 million in US dollars and would assist in leadership training and establish the managing organization for the teams implementing smart ports/smart harbors strategies in three locations. The CANAM

Smart Ports and Harbors Program would solicit grants to establish three port/harbor zones, two in Canada and one in the United States. The three port/harbor zones are at risk due to rising sea levels. The disruption to any of the zones will have devastating impact economically and socially for millions of people.

The three coastal zones selected to receive CANAM Smart Ports and Harbors Program grant awards are the Port of Pascagoula and the Harbors of Pascagoula and Biloxi in Mississippi; the Port of Vancouver, British Columbia, Steveston Harbour on the Fraser River, and Nanaimo Harbour on Vancouver Island; and the Port of Halifax and the Harbours of Halifax and Lunenburg in Nova Scotia. All three areas have major ports of commercial shipping significance and multiple commercial fisheries vital to the economic health of the region. Each area has a major naval or coast guard installation nearby. Since all three coastal zones are extremely susceptible to rising sea levels and extreme weather events, grant funds will be used for sustainable infrastructure strategies, technology upgrades, data collection, and robust communication networks. Model solutions and innovations developed by the CANAM Smart Ports and Harbors Program grant awardees will eventually be available to any interested coastal village, town, or city.

The port/harbor zone grant applicants had to sign extensive cooperation agreements with one another before submitting a grant proposal. One major objective of the CANAM Smart Ports and Harbors Program is to establish patterns of cooperation and collaboration between local, regional, state, and federal agencies. Major corporations and small independent business owners such as commercial fishers would be included in any regionalized network developed by the grant. The idea that organizations from such diverse backgrounds could, in fact, work together was a bold step toward addressing rising sea levels, an existential threat to coastal communities. Grant activities would be at risk if turf battles between organizations became the default method for interactions. The CAGIS team had specific training to minimize competition and maximize cooperation between all grant awardees.

The CAGIS Foundation team's participation in the CANAM Smart Ports and Harbors Program would be twofold. First, the CAGIS Foundation team would form the nucleus of a separate managing organization for the program and would select individuals from partner organizations who would be responsible for coordinating all activities. The CAGIS Foundation team members were an ideal choice for leading the separate managing support organization, given their myriad experiences in maritime logistics, success in establishing attainable goals with timelines, and effective communication skills. They understood that putting structures in place for coordinating activities, collecting information, and communicating with grant partners and officials from the three coastal zone areas in North America would require focused effort for the success of the project.

Second, the CAGIS Foundation team would provide leadership training for all participating organizations to form a common purpose and focus on agreed-upon tangible goals. A group identity would need to be formed among and between the grantees that include an understanding of each grant partner's contributions. The newly formed project team would need to support one another by engaging in ongoing group experiences that emphasize and build interdependence. The CAGIS Foundation team believed that dispositional thinking is precisely the leadership approach needed for the CANAM Smart Ports and Harbors Program. Marit-Abril remembers reflecting on how perfectly the rationale that motivated the development of the CAGIS *Dispositions of Leadership* was aligned with the needs and purposes of the CANAM Smart Ports and Harbors Program and its new grantees. Embedded within the five *Dispositions of Leadership* are capabilities and practices for accomplishing the focus areas of the CANAM Smart Ports and Harbors Program.

The CAGIS Foundation team brainstormed various ideas for the delivery of this critical leadership training for the grant awardees from each of the three coastal zones. Marit-Abril noted the importance of shared, in-person experiences for forming the needed group identity and for establishing the types of interrelationships and interdependence critical to the success of the CANAM Smart Ports and Harbors Program. The four other CAGIS team members agreed and thoughtfully discussed the goals and purposes of the training. Marit-Abril suggested a five-day trip at sea, with each day of the journey focused on one of the five *Dispositions of Leadership*. The other CAGIS team members wholeheartedly endorsed this idea, and Nora noted that it was quite fitting that this leadership training would occur while they were at sea.

CAGIS Team Shakedown Cruise in the Timonerie (Wheelhouse)

The CAGIS team used donated space in the Vancouver offices of Sainte-Foy Marine, Ltd. The office was within easy walking distance of Shipbuilders' Square and Lonsdale Quay Market on the North Shore Waterfront. The CAGIS team met in the technology center office, nicknamed the Wheelhouse (Timonerie in French) for its semicircular shape reminiscent of the bridge of a ship. The room was equipped with smart technology and wall-mounted QD-LCD monitors above the magnificent bank of windows that encased the entire room. The view was stunning, taking in the iconic Q Tower, a landmark for locating Lonsdale Quay Market, Vancouver Harbor, and the beautiful skyline of downtown Vancouver.

The CAGIS team of Marit-Abril Hansen, Erika Knudsen, Nora Jensen, Lincoln Angiak, and Jean-Philippe Gagnon gathered in the Wheelhouse to do a simulated *shakedown cruise* three weeks before the CANAM Smart Ports and Harbors Program grant participants would embark on their five-day leadership training cruise aboard the RV *Smart Ports* (RV designation indicates a research vessel). During the four months preceding the meeting at the Wheelhouse, the CAGIS Foundation team had communicated and exchanged ideas through web-based tools and videoconferencing. All documents were posted on a secure website, with team members posting their work to labeled folders. However, they had all agreed that this face-to-face meeting at the Wheelhouse was prudent to review the final agendas, provide a final critique of all materials, and finalize planning for the five-day sea trip.

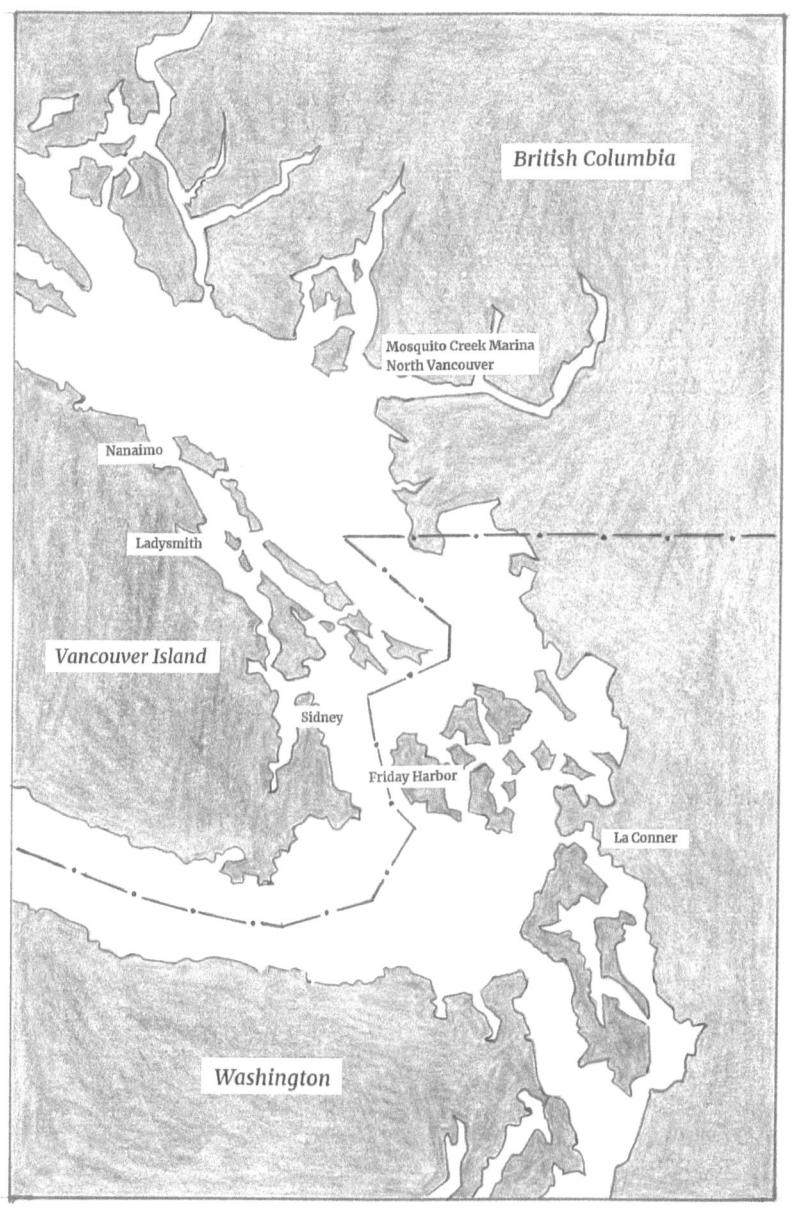

Itinerary for the Five-Day Voyage of Discovery

The CAGIS Foundation team developed a schedule to provide training for grant participants during the day aboard the RV *Smart Ports*. The five-day journey would feature one disposition each day in the floating learning lab. The participants sleep and have breakfast at selected hotels, lodges, or a local bed and breakfast in each port of call. Lunch and snacks are provided aboard the RV *Smart Ports*. Professional event planners arranged all meals, lodging, and transportation to Vancouver. Two professional editors and a publication specialist with web expertise handled the distribution of all training materials. A retired BC Ferries captain was responsible for charting, sailing, and staffing the crew for the RV *Smart Ports*. The CAGIS Foundation team needed to focus on the leadership training and relationship-building of the grant participants, so hired professionals would attend to the other important details for the journey.

The leadership training would be structured around the CAGIS *Dispositions of Leadership*, with one disposition being covered each of the five days. The first letter of each disposition creates the name CAGIS, the foundation seeking to create a better world through visionary leadership. The specific itinerary aboard the RV *Smart Ports*, including the disposition to be taught and the daily sailing destination, was:

Day 1: *Communicating to Understand and to Influence*, from Mosquito Creek Marina in North Vancouver via Nanaimo to Ladysmith, all in British Columbia;

Day 2: *Interdependent Thinking and Acting*, Ladysmith to Sidney, British Columbia;

Day 3: *Gathering Information for Improvement and Innovation*, Sidney to Friday Harbor, Washington;

Day 4: *Seeking Support and Feedback*, Friday Harbor to La Conner Harbor, Washington;

Day 5: *Adaptive Competence*, La Conner Harbor back to Mosquito Creek Marina.

Marit-Abril, Nora, Erika, Lincoln, and Jean-Philippe acknowledged during their conversations at the Wheelhouse that the order of presentation of the five *Dispositions of Leadership* did not strictly follow the mnemonic name CAGIS. In a lighthearted but partially serious manner, given her pedantic tendencies, Marit-Abril wondered aloud if they should rename the foundation CIGSA to better match their itinerary for the five-day leadership training. As they had already registered as a charitable foundation with the Canada Revenue Service (CRA), the easier course was obviously to rearrange the leadership training presentations. But all team members agreed that the planned order of the presentations was a better way to introduce the grant participants to each of the dispositions, even if it did not spell CAGIS. Plus, as Lincoln quickly pointed out to his teammates, this would be a quick lesson for participants on flexibility and adaptability!

A detailed map would be provided to each participant because the voyage covered one of the three coastal zones selected to participate in the CANAM Smart Ports and Harbors Program: the Port of Vancouver, Steveston Harbour on the Fraser River, and Nanaimo Harbour.

Marit-Abril, Lincoln, Nora, Erika, and Jean-Philippe believed that the training would assist all participants in forming strong bonds with one another. They believed that by acting collaboratively and thoughtfully, the entire CANAM Smart Ports and Harbors Program team would accomplish difficult goals that often elude independent-minded individuals seeking personal recognition and reward. The CAGIS Foundation team hoped the five *Dispositions of Leadership* would provide a common mindset and a common language for the participants from the organizations participating in the grant.

The CAGIS team had agreed that each member would be responsible for presenting one disposition and that other team members would assist if requested. Each team member would describe who they are and what they have accomplished. On the day of each designated disposition's presentation, Marit-Abril, Lincoln, Nora, Erika, or Jean-Philippe would briefly share their professional experiences and describe the expertise available to the participants. Each team member would present information in a similar pattern so participants would be able to identify key ideas. The identified disposition would be presented as follows: (1) a brief definition of the identified disposition (what); (2) a rationale (why); and the capabilities and practices (how).

Finally, a brief description each day of the harbor-to-harbor route would *contextualize* the CAGIS *Dispositions of Leadership*. As noted, the participants would be able to see and experience one of the three CANAM Smart Ports and Harbors Program coastal grant zones. The CAGIS Leadership training participants would engage in a dialogue on their first day aboard the RV *Smart Ports* and would be asked to identify their mutual interests and concerns. However, Marit-Abril Hansen would instruct participants to temporarily set aside any suggestions or recommendations until they had a more complete picture of the Port of Vancouver coastal zone.

The leadership team intended to engage training participants in practices around each of the five dispositions in a way that would foster a group identity and build interdependence during their five-day voyage.

CHAPTER ONE:
Questions to Engage Your Thinking and for Discussion or Dialogue with Colleagues

---

The CAGIS Foundation team believed in-person experiences were important for the leadership training participants, as well as for the CAGIS Foundation team in finalizing the details of the leadership training in-person at the Wheelhouse.

1. Why do you think the CAGIS Foundation team members believed that in-person experiences are warranted and necessary?

2. From your own professional experiences, in what ways have the processes and results of in-person meetings differed from those conducted remotely via web-based technology? Why?

One major objective of the CANAM Smart Ports and Harbors Program is to establish patterns of cooperation and collaboration between local, regional, state, and federal agencies.

3. What obstacles or barriers do you foresee in establishing these patterns of cooperation and collaboration between local, regional, state, and federal agencies? How can leadership training help minimize these obstacles and barriers?

Before presenting each day, the designated CAGIS Foundation team member chose to describe who they are and what they have accomplished, including providing a brief description of their formative work experiences, the expertise available to the team, and several important persons responsible for influencing personal and professional growth.

4. Why do you think the CAGIS Foundation team decided to provide this type of personal information before presenting the disposition of the day?

5. When you have delivered presentations, to what extent have you included this type of personal introduction about "Who I Am"?

6. In what ways do you think it would be beneficial to incorporate this type of personal background into future presentations?

Chapter Two

DAY ONE—Introduction and Communicating to Understand and to Influence, from Mosquito Creek Marina-North Vancouver via Nanaimo to Ladysmith

Marit-Abril Hansen Presents

I am Marit-Abril Hansen, and I have the privilege of launching us on a *voyage of discovery* aboard the RV *Smart Ports*, a vessel retrofitted with a hybrid propulsion system. RV is the designation for a research vessel. We will be underway in about 15 minutes as we cruise from Mosquito Creek Marina here in North Vancouver via Nanaimo to Ladysmith. On behalf of the CAGIS team, I invite you to consider the next five days as a voyage of discovery. It is our fervent hope that you *discover* ways to work as a highly productive team and learn ways to be an inclusive and effective leader. We recognize this requires a willingness to be vulnerable in a supportive and trusting environment. The CAGIS team will strive to create conditions for you to make our voyage a profound opportunity to learn about yourself and your team members. Please lean into the experience.

There is a document on each of your tables for our first activity of the morning. Please introduce yourself to three other participants who are not on your team and record their name and favorite meal on the document. We will begin each day by getting to know other participants using this type of activity. This is an *inclusion activity* in which everyone will have a response to the question. There is no right or wrong answer.

I have three specific tasks today: to share our mission, to introduce you to the five CAGIS *Dispositions of Leadership*, and to present the first disposition, Communicating to Understand and to Influence. The CANAM Smart Ports and Harbors Program mission is in Textbox 1, and it will appear throughout most of the materials we share with you.

Textbox 1. CANAM *Smart Ports and Harbors Program* Mission

> Our collective mission is to reduce the impact of severe weather events and rising sea levels on our immediate communities by developing and implementing sustainable and adaptable practices. We will collaborate and network to share our knowledge and insights with one another to improve our plans and the outcomes for our communities.

Overview of Dispositions of Leadership

The *Dispositions of Leadership* provide decision-makers with a multifaceted repertoire of capabilities and practices drawn from rational, emotional, social, and collective intelligent thinking. The five *Dispositions of Leadership* provide a framework for a mutual understanding and approach to our work together. People are not necessarily born with dispositions. They are learned over time, under our control, and we must choose to utilize them consciously and intentionally. The dispositions can be taught, modeled, and learned by any grant participant.

When you and your team are confronted with an array of complex problems as grant decision-makers, you should first decide what thinking is useful before taking any action. Your thinking should be strategic and your actions methodical. Three important ideas about the *Dispositions of Leadership* that I want to include:

- *Capabilities and practices*: The five dispositions are organized with the requisite capabilities and practices. The capabilities and practices were selected from expansive lists and refined to a manageable number of choices for immediate application. The dispositions, capabilities, and practices are not hierarchical in importance, even though they are taught sequentially.[6]

- *There are no automatic scripts*: Utilizing dispositions is contingent upon understanding the situation and the circumstances. It requires decision-makers to constantly diagnose, monitor, and adjust their thinking and actions. The five *Dispositions of Leadership* provide a framework with a manageable number of options and choices.[7]

- *Dispositions are the integration and application of practices and skills*: For example, effective listening begins with being alert when it is needed. Listening to understand combines the practice of attending to what is said with the skill of paraphrasing accurately the information that is received.[8]

Most of your decisions as individuals and teams participating in the CANAM Smart Ports and Harbors Program will be responses to multiple sources of information that require diagnosing the situation before determining a potential course of action. When you are confronted with a situation, you will be called upon to set priorities, draw upon prior knowledge and experiences, weigh the options, and then set a course of action that will impact your respective coastal communities. Addressing complex problems, such as rising sea levels, cannot be addressed with command-and-control leadership practices designed in the previous century to control information and direct people.

It is important for all decision-makers in the grant to understand that leaders and group members are encouraged to utilize or acquire both thinking dispositions and corresponding skillful practices. The first disposition we will explore is *Communicating to Understand and to Influence*. The CAGIS team placed understanding before *influence* because we will be interacting in our respective communities and are encouraged to manage the impulse of speaking before listening. Our credibility and effectiveness in working *with* communities where lifestyles and livelihoods are threatened by rising sea levels will depend on a willingness to be attentive listeners and use the skills to listen effectively.

About Marit-Abril Hansen

Before I go any further, I wanted to provide a very brief background about myself, as will my other four colleagues when they begin each day. My father's heritage is Norwegian, and my mother's Argentinian. Tobias and Camilla Hansen, my parents, showed me that I can benefit from understanding the blessings of two cultures, two worldviews. I grew up commercial fishing, and I have lived an aqueous life as a tugboat captain. I have an Unlimited Master's license, and I can operate any oceangoing vessel. I was fortunate to grow up in an environment where competence, compassion, and empathy were equal foundational pillars of my extended family. I am here today because of the numerous wonderful role models and mentors who took an interest in my personal and professional development.

I attended the California Maritime Academy in Vallejo, California. It was the spring semester of my second year when I met Jean-Philippe at Cal Maritime as part of a sponsored event featuring him as a guest presenter and faculty-in-residence. Jean-Philippe Gagnon, CEO of Sainte-Foy Marine, Ltd., was selected because he is considered a *thought leader* in the maritime industry. Jean-Philippe has been a friend, mentor, and colleague ever since I heard his presentation "Who I Am, Who Will You Become, and What Might We Address for the Future of the Maritime Industry?"

His presentation was a profound experience which I have used as a touchstone for many aspects of my personal and professional life.

I see myself as having a strong inner core and a peaceful and reserved outer core. My demeanor has served me well. A thoughtful and decisive approach is needed when the demands of operating a vessel in imminent danger might cost the lives of your crew.

I would like you to consider placing aside your current beliefs about leadership, as I have had to, and consider an approach and framework that will serve us in a new and challenging context. We will be compelled to work together because going it alone is not an option for our endangered coastal zone communities.

The Days Ahead

The RV *Smart Ports* is motoring from Mosquito Harbour to Nanaimo because both communities are part of the CANAM Smart Ports and Harbors Program identified as the Vancouver Harbour coastal zone. You have a detailed nautical chart of our five-day journey in the materials. It is anticipated that all three coastal teams will have the opportunity to share vital information about their communities. Today, the Vancouver Harbour coastal team will introduce themselves during lunch and provide a 15-minute overview of their work plan during dinner this evening.

We will have extensive interaction time each day within and between teams to create the conditions whereby we will hopefully develop into a collaborative and supportive team. High-functioning teams capable of addressing complex problems do not just occur. As I mentioned a few minutes ago, the CAGIS team strives to create the conditions to develop and grow. We will encourage you to read the information provided each day and interact as a *home group* and with members from other groups sharing this journey with you. All materials, including PowerPoints, will be available on the web. Our open-source policy serves as both a resource bank for you to use when interacting in your respective communities and as an avenue for improving all materials and processes.

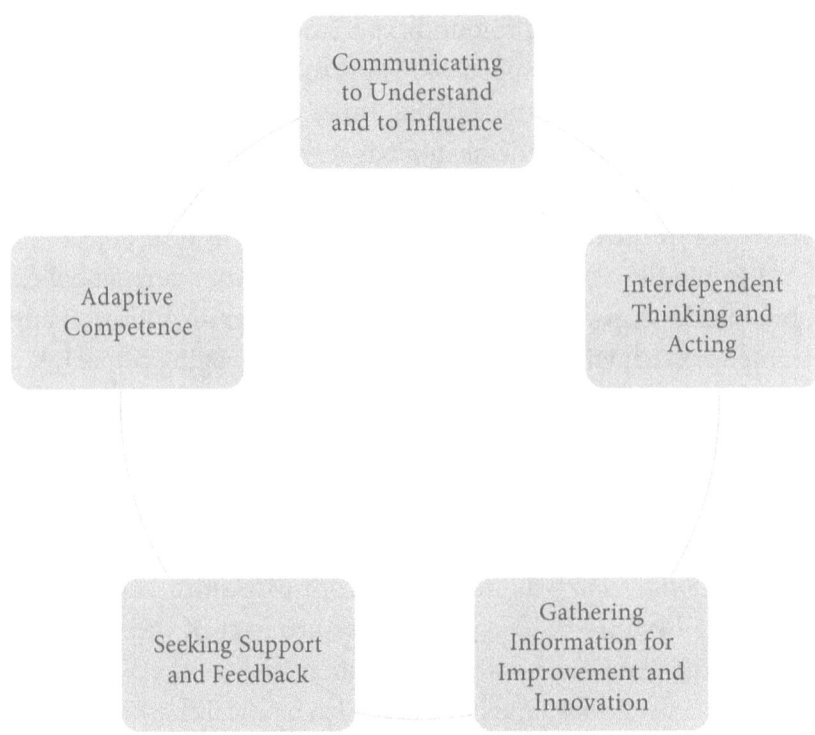

The Five Dispositions of Leadership

The CAGIS Foundation team believes that the five *Dispositions of Leadership* provide an innovative framework for individual and team development. The dispositions are not hierarchical, meaning they have equal importance. We will start at the twelve o'clock position and work our way clockwise through each of the five *Dispositions of Leadership*. The dispositions will be taught sequentially because specific team practices lead to effective group performance. Each day will feature one disposition.

Disposition: Communicating to Understand and to Influence

Today we will start our leadership voyage with the disposition Communicating to Understand and to Influence. It has been our experience as the CAGIS Foundation team that effective communication skills must be in place *before* addressing complex problems. The two capabilities are arranged in a deliberate sequence. We encourage you to consider interacting in productive ways as individuals and then transitioning to effective ways for working as teams and with groups. We have identified the capabilities as Developing Personal Presence and Cultivating Productive Working Relationships, as noted in Table 1. The practices learned in Developing Personal Presence have direct applicability when using the practices noted in Cultivating Productive Working Relationships.

A major goal of the grant is to engage local communities in efforts to address the impact of rising sea levels. We are *front-loading* materials that provide strategies and processes for working with groups. Engagement with local communities is a goal that many organizations do poorly. Your team will likely be judged favorably by initial efforts if those impacted the most feel heard and respected. The information we will provide has *dual-track* possibilities. It can be used with your team and when you engage in a public process. Local communities must be engaged and committed to any solutions if the effects of rising sea levels are addressed at scale in your entire geographic area. It will be time consuming and challenging to create a mindset that we are all in this together. An alternative is that the perception will emerge that a plan was created by outside experts and imposed by those who do not have a vested interest in local communities.

The practices and strategies you will learn when interacting with the Cultivating Productive Working Relationships materials are like navigational aids for safe guidance used while sailing the RV *Smart Ports*. It is our responsibility to prepare you well so that you will avoid common pitfalls when engaging members of your community and avoid a messy spectacle of running aground in public.

Table 1. Disposition: Communicating to Understand and to Influence

CAPABILITY: Developing Personal Presence (you)
PRACTICES:
• Know and create conditions for being personally present (place aside distractions, monitor breathing)
• Be aware and alert to situations and contexts that require attentive listening
• Listen with undivided attention and empathy (monitor body language)
• Pause (demonstrate listening)
• Paraphrase (demonstrate understanding)
• Reframe negative language and model positivity
• Respond non-defensively and avoid sarcasm
CAPABILITY: Cultivating Productive Working Relationships (you and others)
PRACTICES:
• Establish norms for interacting and communicating
• Develop working agreements and agendas
• Use discussion protocols and strategies for balanced participation
• Utilize strategies for encouraging dialogue and discussion
• Recognize and include diverse backgrounds and cultural perspectives
• Manage conflict proactively for healthy outcomes

Capability: Developing Personal Presence

"Personal presence involves having heightened levels of self-awareness and social awareness because human interactions are dynamic and situational."[9] An initial step as an effective communicator is to develop personal presence by creating routines and conditions for being calm and focused while in social settings. We need to discover how to place aside distractions and control our breathing to be relaxed and focused. It is helpful to identify and prioritize the most important communication and select the time and place for a thoughtful response.

An attribute of effective communicators is to learn to "read" situations, make necessary adjustments in the moment, and select from a repertoire of interpersonal skills and strategies. We should strive to acknowledge comments that are made while realizing that not all comments require a response. Effective communicators strive to be composed in preparation for an upcoming interaction or when transitioning from an emotionally taxing situation. Maintaining a personal presence in social settings can be inhibited by becoming defensive or taking criticism too personally. It is difficult to let go of comments made by others that are not useful in the moment.

There are two helpful approaches that avoid the common interpersonal pitfall of conversations devolving into unproductive, negative, or heated exchanges. First, focus initially on creating an understanding rather than striving to justify, persuade, convince, or convert others to adopt one's point of view. Creating an understanding is about listening to others' thoughts and inquiring about what might be the beliefs or values that inform their point of view. Second, the interpersonal communication skills of pausing, paraphrasing, and inquiring into the thinking of others are tools for maintaining positive and open communication. Fortunately, there is almost always time to craft a thoughtful response and reminding oneself of this simple fact might inhibit an impulsive and regrettable comment.

Effective communicators model positivity. We are convinced that positivity is an essential characteristic of team effectiveness. Positivity in our context affirms the belief that team members possess the capabilities and resourcefulness to accomplish the challenges in front of them. Modeling an optimistic view sets the tone for how a team will respond when they are discouraged or encounter setbacks. Negativity inhibits a team from engaging in sustained and creative thinking. We assert that sustained and creative thinking will be critical as we respond to the consequences of rising sea levels for our respective coastal zone communities. Healthy skepticism is unlike negativity because it strengthens assumptions by compelling us to ask difficult questions and provide evidence.

During the next five days, we will have activities to practice pausing, paraphrasing, and creating an understanding by not responding defensively or attempting to persuade. We will provide the opportunity to put all these practices together by learning to reframe negative comments. Applying the seven practices bulleted under the capability Developing Personal Presence requires a nuanced approach. Table 2 is a sample comment pattern, which we will use as a model during activities.

Table 2. Sample Comment Pattern

Team member (statement)	"I think learning about personal presence is unnecessary, and we just need to get to work."
Facilitator (paraphrase)	"You believe learning about personal presence is a waste of your time."

Team member (statement)	"Absolutely."
Facilitator (response)	"I view it differently, and I have found that by developing effective communication skills, a team is better equipped to address complex problems and develop possible solutions."

In private life and in professional settings, we need to recognize that being liked by everyone is unrealistic and a bar set too high. Learning to live with the knowledge that some people will not like us because we are in a professional role is difficult. The disposition of Communicating to Understand and to Influence compels us to take the high road and focus on what will positively influence others. Sarcastic comments either escalate an interaction or silence individuals who will now opt to remain quiet. If you have convinced yourself that an impulsive comment makes you feel good *in the moment*, consider not saying it. Personal presence is maintaining poise and calm while managing our emotions and impulses to react or respond.

Capability: Cultivating Productive Working Relationships

To address the objectives of the CANAM Smart Ports and Harbors Program, we will need to design a work environment that fosters continuous learning whereby grant partners can begin to collaboratively solve complex problems. This is a major departure from many organizational cultures that have a defined hierarchy, with a manager or management team organizing and directing subordinates. Many of us might feel unprepared for and overwhelmed by the challenges of organizing and working with diverse groups representing many organizations.

Four of the five CAGIS team members are well acquainted with commanding vessels that have clear lines of authority and a hierarchy defined by rank and status. We would all tell you that the leadership skills needed for *being in command* aboard vessels in the saltwater do not necessarily apply to many situations away from our vessels when they are firmly grounded on dry land. It has been a learning curve for us to consider developing an innovative leadership framework that requires learning new ways of being and doing.

In particular, the practices for Cultivating Productive Working Relationships have added to our repertoire of leadership skills. We encourage you to think of the practices and skills you will learn as acquiring new strategies that add to the skills you currently use and depend upon. A common theme woven throughout our work together is to develop the capacity for strategically applying *both/and* thinking as opposed to *either/or* thinking.

We encourage you to use the seven practices from Developing Personal Presence and utilize them to cultivate working relationships. Our team will use a set of four norms each time we convene meetings with grant partners. These norms are foundational for interacting and communicating in a constructive manner. We recommend that your team consider utilizing the CANAM Norms Defined described in Table 3.[10]

These four critical practices that enhance team interpersonal communication are:

- Listening to understand
- Acknowledging equal status and striving for balanced participation
- Proceeding with transparency and openness
- Supporting colleagues and disagreeing with ideas, not people

The four norms were carefully selected for two specific reasons. First, the norms will create predictability about what to expect at all our convenings and certainty for how we, as the CAGIS Foundation team, will interact with all participants. Second, each team participating in the CANAM Smart Ports and Harbors Program will be meeting with communities that are profoundly impacted by rising sea levels. We anticipate that you will encounter people who are frustrated, disenfranchised, and even suspicious of your motives. The norms will increase the odds of creating an environment that communicates *we are in this together and invite you to participate as equals because we all have a stake in what happens*. It is almost impossible to overcome an adversarial relationship once it is established.

Table 3. CANAM Norms Defined

Listening to	Attending intently to what is said conveys we are listening
Understand	Paraphrasing communicates we understood what was said
Acknowledging Equal Status and	Establishing an environment where no participant has more or less value in the community
Striving for Balanced Participation	Providing all members of the community with equal and balanced opportunities to make comments or contributions

Proceeding with Transparency and Openness	Ensuring that actions and decisions are made in front of and with the entire team

Temporarily placing aside opinions and being willing to consider the ideas of other team members |
| Supporting Colleagues and

Disagreeing with Ideas, not People | Committing to assist and encourage other team members when invited

Constructively critiquing assertions or ideas without being critical of colleagues themselves |

Table 3 CANAM Norms Defined provides a starting point for the activities you will be asked to complete with your home group. We will begin each day by suggesting that your home group identifies one norm to focus on for the day. Time will be allotted for your home group to refine or adjust the terminology in Table 3 so it makes sense to you. We caution you not to add to the list of norms before we introduce the idea of *working agreements*.[11]

Our team would like to provide some background about why we spend time with the CANAM Norms for Productive Collaboration. A productive and positive work setting has an environment that is safe and predictable. This environment is constructed so group members feel emotionally safe and capable of engaging in work that is difficult and might lead to discomfort.

Placing emotion in a positive context allows individuals and groups to engage in complex cognitive work. Emotion plays an important role when learning new and challenging information.

It plays an even more significant role when we are asked to make changes to our behaviors or even to our belief system. We recognize that we will be gathering and managing enormous amounts of information that will require focused cognitive engagement. Our work will not be complete by simply analyzing and sharing information.

We are tasked with creating and implementing solutions that involve multiple agencies, organizations, and citizens from all walks of life. This will require intense emotional engagement. The CAGIS Foundation team aspires to develop a work environment that is intentional and recognizes that cognition and emotion are intertwined, albeit often artificially separated. We will be well served by understanding how we might collectively influence social engagement for positive outcomes.

Develop Working Agreements and Agendas

The CANAM Norms for Productive Collaboration are used during all convenings, and all grant partners are encouraged to use them. Each team develops working agreements to accomplish work effectively and efficiently. It is recommended that you create three to five statements that summarize the key needs of the work team. Working agreements are designed to avoid actions and behaviors that inhibit the functioning of the group. Not all teams or groups will develop the same set of working agreements because their needs or concerns will be different. A team might develop a working agreement about staying focused or using time efficiently. These two topics might be nonissues for another team, so it would not include time use or focus in its set of working agreements.

The CAGIS team recommends that a working agreement is stated succinctly and positively. Table 4 describes a working agreement we have developed in the past. A sample worksheet and a list of possible topics for developing working agreements will be available during a home group activity.

Table 4. Sample Working Agreement

Be Present	Colleagues have our full attention, no sidebar conversations, monitor body language; appropriate use of technology by agreement, such as cell phones are silent, queue text messages, computers are used for notetaking (critical or emergency contact is exempted)
Use Time Wisely	Be on time, start on time, end on time, honor allotted time for each agenda item; turn-taking is respected, so we all have time (time bandits and oxygen pirates only make appearances in the movies)

The CAGIS team recommends the use of meeting agendas. The information presented can be used as a starting point for adopting components of meeting agendas or for improving agendas your team already uses. Agendas are critical for predictability, focus, and efficient use of time. Agendas can be open for any team member to add a topic, topics can be submitted to a team leader for review, or the agenda can be developed as a group. An effective way to distribute the workload for any meeting or convening is to utilize meeting roles. It has been the experience of the CAGIS Foundation team that engagement at meetings increases when team members share the responsibilities and are committed to successful meeting processes and outcomes. Four sample meeting roles are described in Table 5.[12]

Table 5. Team Member Meeting Roles

Facilitator	Actively runs the meeting with an agreed upon agenda, maintains protocols and success criteria to be used, and reminds the team
Information Organizer	Organizes the agenda and distributes materials and documents physically or electronically for the meeting
Recorder and Disseminator	Collects completed work products, takes summary notes, and distributes summary notes to team members
Timekeeper and Process Observer	Times agenda topics, documents agreed upon team skills such as paraphrasing, reports out to the team how many times a skill was used (no names), leads team reflection

The objectives of the CANAM Smart Ports and Harbors Program require that grant partners communicate frequently and share information transparently. This, of course, can happen in real time, face-to-face, virtually, and asynchronously when meetings are not scheduled. However, given that grant partners are in three different time zones in North America, meeting with predictable frequency will be essential regionally for coordinating activities and sharing insights into what is being learned. Convenings will also be scheduled with all grant partners, although less frequently than regional partner meetings. The CAGIS Foundation team suggests we commit to having effective meetings that partners look forward to rather than the type of dread we experience when meetings are perceived as ineffective and a waste of time.

Time is a valuable resource, and meetings should be held when necessary and have a clear purpose. Meetings should be well facilitated, structured for balanced participation, and have clearly stated goals, outcomes, and success criteria. It has been our experience that meetings held via web-based platforms should have the same elements as face-to-face meetings. The structure of a meeting is important, and it defines specific expectations for how a group will do their work. The Elements of an Effective Meeting are identified in Table 6.

Table 6. Elements of an Effective Meeting

Agenda Developed and Distributed	Agendas are distributed well in advance; topics are realistic and prioritized given the allotted time; agendas state who is responsible for each agenda item; processes or protocols to be used are identified; items to bring and items to read or review before meeting are identified sufficiently in advance; and any hot topics are placed at the end of the agenda.
Meeting Processes, Outcomes, and Success Criteria	Norms and working agreements are visible when the meeting begins; why and how a protocol will be used will be explicitly noted; how participants can contribute will be described; outcomes and meeting success criteria are noted and transparent.

Effectively Run Meeting	Facilitator manages the selected processes of the meeting and redirects and refocuses others when needed; the process observer manages time and records data selected by the team (e.g., turn taking); the recorder takes summary notes and distributes them.
Meeting Conclusion	The team reviews meeting outcomes, decisions, products, and tasks to be completed; team members briefly discuss the effectiveness of the norms, working agreements, protocols, and success criteria before concluding the meeting. (Note: Teams that do not reflect are less likely to learn as a team.)

Discussion and Dialogue

Discussion is the most common form of group conversation. Discussion is used to propose solutions, prioritize, identify potential decisions, and select a course of action.[13] Discussion is a convergent process because it is designed to eliminate choices to move forward with a focus. One crucial element to include in discussions is to identify who has the decision-making authority *before* beginning the discussion. For example, will the decision be made by team consensus, a simple majority vote, a supermajority of 75 percent of the participants, or by leaders of an organization from three rank-ordered choices submitted to them? Ultimately, the support for a decision begins with *clarity* about the decision-making process and *identifying* who has the decision-making authority.[14]

The CAGIS Norms for Productive Meetings and Working Agreements are critical to use when a team has a discussion. The Elements of an Effective Meeting should be used during a discussion, so the meeting is well organized and efficiently managed, and so the team has ample time to make decisions. It is more likely that team members will commit to moving forward and support a decision if the process used to make decisions is believed to be transparent and fair. It is essential that a decision is supported by all participants, even though during the process, some members may have preferred a different outcome. Transparency and fairness in this context really matter to preserve a healthy group identity.

Dialogue is a conversation type that is underutilized, misunderstood, and often unwittingly combined with a decision-making process. Dialogue is a divergent process that explores choices or creates an understanding, and it does not conclude with a decision.[15] Groups that address complex problems need to view dialogue as an essential group process skill to explore ideas, options, and potential solutions. It is hoped that CANAM Smart Ports teams will learn to deeply examine options to improve decisions.

The CAGIS team believes the capabilities and practices introduced earlier are vital for a successful dialogue. How conversations are structured, the verbal skillfulness of participants, and the way participants regard one another will all influence whether a group can effectively explore how to solve complex problems and address adaptive challenges.

Dialogue is a type of disciplined conversation, and the purpose is for participants to examine assumptions and construct meaning. Teams that learn new interpersonal communication skills will enhance the quality of dialogue. Interpersonal communication skills used during the discussion are the same as those used in dialogue. However, skills are selected to support the dialogue process specifically and to illuminate an important feature of the relationship between all participants: equal status. For example, it might be useful to agree that all members of the team have an opportunity to speak once before any member speaks a second time. It is a misconception that the contributions of a team member assigned higher positional authority than other group members are somehow more useful.

The success of dialogue begins with the idea that team members all have equal status. Dialogue is a form of conversation that is nonjudgmental, nonevaluative, and nonhierarchical. It is a foundational group process that has the potential for creating mutual understanding and strengthening group identity. A dialogue is not a process for defending or critiquing ideas, judging the veracity of a team member's thinking, or asserting positional authority.

The intention of *dialogue* is to create a *mutually shared understanding* and *not to decide* on a course of action. This often makes some group members uncomfortable, particularly task-oriented individuals. However, dialogue is not a rudderless journey whereby sharing ideas is both the process and the product. It is helpful to remind team members that even though a decision will not be made, there is a destination: making detailed sense of all available information and clarity about potential options. The processes used for dialogue need to be inclusive so that all members of the team develop shared meaning. Organizations often skip dialogue because of the belief that there is not enough time to invest in such a process. When dialogue is skipped, the CAGIS Foundation team has observed that organizations continue to revisit the same item multiple times during a *discussion process* because the decisions do not land on solid footing with those designated to implement.

Dialogue is a process that can be used to describe and understand the elements of a complex challenge. Participants intentionally avoid offering interpretations of their experiences and avoid offering solutions prematurely. A dialogue should result in clarity of the potential options through understanding what they are and function as a catalyst for moving forward. Skillful facilitators will redirect and defer interpretations or solutions to another time designated for a discussion. An effective team places *equal value on discussion and dialogue* and recognizes why, when, and how to utilize each conversation type.

Feedback for Improving Team Performance

The CAGIS team believes that many organizations build employee evaluation processes that are hierarchical, with a supervisor collecting and delivering performance information to a subordinate for promotion or financial compensation purposes. Information collected by a team participating in the CANAM Smart Ports and Harbor Program is not for employment decisions. We have discovered that personnel evaluation processes are so ingrained in many organizations that it is challenging to establish processes that are designed to improve overall team performance. Teams participating in the CANAM Smart Ports and Harbor Program should not be evaluated against an external personnel performance standard since this encourages unnecessary and detrimental competition. The CAGIS team has adopted two practices that reduce defensiveness and the human inclination to take feedback personally. First, a team should assess its performance based on agreed upon criteria. Second, selecting a predetermined schedule to assess performance will alert all members that a review is not a reflexive response to conflict, but part of the team's ongoing commitment to growth.

Since feedback in a collegial setting is a mutual decision made in advance by a team for growth and improved performance, the information used needs to be *fact-based*, *nonjudgmental*, and *communicated professionally*.[16] Feedback on team performance should be routine and not be considered occasional or idiosyncratic. A commitment to regularly collecting and processing predetermined information should be built into a team meeting schedule and part of agendas that are developed. For example, the Elements of an Effective Meeting (Table 6) establish steps for a process observer to collect information and time for the team to determine how effectively they utilized a process or a skill. A team might decide to collect information on how effectively an agenda was followed and if balanced participation was achieved.

The CAGIS Foundation team believes that team formation and identity should focus initially on learning and utilizing the practices described in Cultivating Productive Working Relationships. We have learned that it is ill-advised for teams to immediately analyze data or implement grant goals before establishing the practices and skills that support team success. Teams can become discouraged or disillusioned if they have difficulty overcoming challenges because feedback is designed to be critical and not supportive.

Recognize and Include Diverse Backgrounds and Cultural Perspectives

There are moral, social, and practical reasons to care about diversity. The moral reason for diversity is that groups ignored, overlooked, or underrepresented should have a voice and equal status in a community. The social reason for diversity is groups that are created need to strive for a demographic composition representative of their community. The practical reason for diverse groups, if created thoughtfully, is they are more capable of designing innovations and solving complex problems than are less diverse groups. The CAGIS Foundation team would like you to know that we have had to grapple with maximizing the benefits and addressing the challenges of being a diverse group. All grant partners have indicated a commitment to the objectives of the grant without exploring what that precisely means to us as a larger community.

The CANAM Smart Ports and Harbors Program has brought together a group of diverse organizations and individuals. Each has established values and possibly different approaches for addressing challenges. We are a newly formed team because of, not despite, our diverse backgrounds and cultural perspectives. The CAGIS team recommends that we anticipate the challenges faced by diverse groups by (1) developing a strong group identity, (2) enhancing effective interpersonal communication and strategies, and (3) utilizing strategies for minimizing nonproductive conflict. A team of diverse individuals will overcome potential differences by being committed to overall team success and by recognizing, understanding, and appreciating the contributions of other organizations and individuals.

We have already introduced and examined structures and strategies that, if implemented effectively, will support us in addressing and resolving our differences. By anticipating the challenges of creating diverse teams and putting norms, working agreements, and processes into place, we hope to maximize the benefits while moderating the challenges. The CAGIS Foundation team understands the need to transition from the aspirational (recognizing the need for diverse teams) to the functional (putting in place useful practices that assist teams to work together effectively).

A productive adult learning environment focused on the development of the CANAM Smart Ports and Harbors Program team is our starting point. Our diverse group will be well served if we choose to be allocentric or focused on our newly formed community, the development of our CANAM team, and the objectives of the grant. We suggest that being idiocentric and focused on our interests is more likely to promote a competitive environment whereby our team will be less receptive to diverse perspectives.[17] The *opportunity* we have as we begin our journey is to create a productive learning environment by expanding our pool of *shared knowledge* and *increasing group competencies,* so we can utilize the benefits of diversity.

The CANAM Norms for Productive Collaboration, the recommendation to create working agreements, team member roles, and the elements of an effective meeting are structures and practices put in place to promote the value of each team member's contributions. The practices in Developing Personal Presence and Cultivating Productive Working Relationships offer opportunities for each team member to understand the positive ways individual actions can contribute to the success of the team. We are diverse in our demographic composition, geographic location, organizational culture, and cultural heritage. These group attributes can lead to our success when we commit to implementing the capabilities and practices we have discussed today. We will all benefit from the positive contributions of a diverse community. The *Strategies to Support Diversity* in Table 7 can temper the effects of misunderstandings arising from diverse perspectives.

Table 7. Strategies to Support Diversity

Establish a Safe Environment	• Ensure psychological safety for all participants
Developing Personal Presence	• Listen with undivided attention and empathy (monitoring body language) • Pause (demonstrate listening) • Paraphrase (demonstrate understanding) • Reframe negative language and model positivity • Respond non-defensively and avoid sarcasm
Cultivating Productive Working Relationships (norms)	• Listen to understand • Acknowledge equal status and strive for balanced participation • Proceed with transparency and openness • Support colleagues and disagree with ideas, not people
Sample Working Agreements	• Be present (attend to all team members) • Use time wisely (take turns)
Extend Thinking and Examine Alternatives	• Advocate the use of *both/and* rather than *either/or* thinking

Use Language Stems for Productive Conflict	• "I have a different take on this topic…" • "I view this from a different vantage point…" • "I don't understand your position, please explain it a little more…" • "I see your point and might we refine it by considering…"

Conflict is a normal part of our professional lives, especially when teams or groups have differences. The challenge for us is to direct conflict toward ideas or potential decisions and away from being directed at individuals or groups. Productive conflict can improve decisions when used constructively. Personal criticism or critical comments directed toward team members are the antitheses of a psychologically safe environment. The strategies noted in Table 7 are useful when addressing situations that have the potential for conflict.

The CAGIS Foundation team suggests we focus on what we can change and not on the unalterable facts that define each of us and make us uniquely wonderful. I would like to share more information about myself that I refrained from discussing earlier because it relates directly to what we are talking about now. I am biracial, with American-Norwegian and Argentinian-Spanish ancestry. I have light brown skin, dark hair, and brown eyes. It has been assumed that since my last name is Norwegian, I should have blonde hair and blue eyes. It is a misconception that all Norwegians are blonde and blue-eyed. My father has dark hair and brown eyes. I have also heard that since I have Argentinian ancestry and am a woman, I am prone to being emotional, even fiery. It has been assumed by some individuals that since I am a sea captain, a woman in a man's profession, I should act like a man—whatever that means. Should I have an overbearing demeanor and a commanding bearing? I am five foot four inches tall, usually quiet, and reserved as a person.

I have captained salmon seine boats and tugboats and served as an officer on container ships. It has been assumed, innocently and ignorantly, that I am probably like some of the stars of *The Deadliest Catch* television program—that I swear, chain smoke, drink coffee nonstop, and while in port, party hardy. I rarely swear, have never smoked, prefer green tea as a hot beverage, and occasionally drink alcohol. I defy easy stereotypes, as we all do. I like who I am, and I am proud of my unique heritage. We should reject stereotypes, biased and unhealthy views often based on unalterable facts, and focus on what we can contribute and what we can change in the challenging work in front of us. The CAGIS team recognizes the unique heritage that informs our insights and the expertise that can be utilized when we create the conditions that invite the benefits of diversity.

Sequencing of Understanding and Influence

The notion of influence was saved until after we explored the practices and behaviors of Communicating to Understand and to Influence. There are two reasons for this sequence. First, it is critical that before we decide to influence others, we should seek to understand them. Second, influence begins by establishing a relationship with others to have a positive effect on their thinking or actions. This relationship-influence model of communication does not rely on exerting positional authority or hierarchical power. The capabilities and practices in this disposition, if used effectively, allow us to establish credibility and possibly influence others when needed. We fervently believe that the capabilities and practices in Communicating to Understand and to Influence are the foundation for establishing relational trust.

Chapter Two:
Questions to Engage Your Thinking
and for Discussion or Dialogue with Colleagues

Communicating to Understand and to Influence focuses initially on creating an understanding rather than striving to justify, persuade, convince, or convert others to adopt one's point of view. Creating an understanding is about listening to others' thoughts and inquiring about what might be the beliefs or values that inform their point of view.

1. In what ways and to what extent do you think understanding others' thoughts, beliefs, and values are critical to communication?

2. For you personally and professionally, what are the obstacles and barriers to Communicating to Understand and to Influence? How can you better understand others' thoughts, beliefs, and values rather than striving to justify, persuade, convince, or convert others to adopt your point of view?

During the training, Marit-Abril asserts that support for a decision begins with *clarity* about the decision-making process and *identifying* who has the decision-making authority *before* beginning the discussion.

3. From your perspective and experience, how important is it for the decision-making authority to be identified before the discussion begins?

4. Can you think of times in your personal or professional life that it would have been beneficial for you to have known

what decision-making process was being used and who had the decision-making authority prior to the discussion beginning? How might this information have changed the discussion and/or supported the decisions made because of the discussion?

Marit-Abril states that the CAGIS Foundation fervently believes that the capabilities and practices in Communicating to Understand and to Influence are the foundation for establishing relational trust.

5. How does Communicating to Understand and to Influence create the foundation for relational trust?

6. Please refer to Appendix A for an opportunity to actively participate as a team member of The Gulf Coast Sea Level Rise Consortium. The consortium represents the Port of Pascagoula, Mississippi, and the Harbors of Pascagoula and Biloxi, Mississippi. The team is deliberating over how to utilize the capabilities and practices from the disposition Communicating to Understand and to Influence.

Chapter Three

DAY TWO—Interdependent Thinking and Acting, from Ladysmith to Sidney

---

Jean-Philippe Gagnon Presents

My name is Jean-Philippe Gagnon. I encouraged the CAGIS Foundation team to begin our journey aboard the RV *Smart Ports*, the floating learning lab, with strategies on how to work together effectively. I offer my thanks to Marit-Abril for providing us with the capabilities and strategies we will use throughout our careers. I learned some difficult lessons leading the *Sleek Surface Maritime* development team, something I will discuss in more depth in a moment. The most difficult lesson I learned was that gathering many task-oriented partners together without first providing the support structures of sound interpersonal communication practices inhibits progress. Given my experiences, I was urged by the CAGIS Foundation team to lead the work today, which focused on the second disposition: *Interdependent Thinking and Acting*.

The CAGIS Foundation team thought it was relevant to provide some background information about ourselves. We were concerned that if we spent too much talking about ourselves, it would take away from developing our collective identity as the CANAM Smart Ports and Harbor Program team. So briefly, here are a few pertinent details about my life to give you a sense of who I am. I lived in both Saint-Jean-Baptiste, Québec, and

Flint, Michigan, as a child and young adult. My mother was killed in an automobile accident when I was only seven years old. My father was a longshoreman at the Port of Québec, and he never recovered from losing his beloved wife. Fortunately, my maternal grandparents in Michigan and paternal grandparents in Québec took a serious interest in my upbringing. I am proudly a Francophone and an Anglophone.

I earned a marine engineering degree at Cape Breton University in Nova Scotia, and I have numerous maritime licenses. I am an executive and founder of Sainte-Foy Marine, Ltd. We are a maritime company with offices and tugboats on the west coast of North America in Vancouver and on the east coast in Québec City. Sainte-Foy Marine has a major presence in the Canadian Arctic Archipelago, supporting the coast guard and navy of our wonderful country. Sainte-Foy Marine has an extensive program to sponsor and provide mentoring assistance for underrepresented groups in the maritime industry. Our company has a moral duty to reduce the environmental impact of our industry and an ethical obligation to help others.

I led the international team that developed *Sleek Surface Maritime*. For those who may not know, *Sleek Surface Maritime* is an environmental-friendly biocide-free hull coating that reduces fuel consumption by minimizing calcium deposits under a ship's paint. It was considered a major innovation because the nontoxic coating improved fuel efficiency by reducing resistance on the hull of a ship. The development team spent five and a half years from the experimental stages to creating a final product. As a team, we were motivated to lessen the environmental impact of our industry. Our development team's commitment was to form a foundation and direct almost all the profits generated by the sale of *Sleek Surface Maritime* to philanthropic pursuits. We are currently applying the lessons learned from developing *Sleek Surface Maritime* to the research and development of green hydrogen to power container ships.

I have co-chaired the Arctic Circle Assembly with Ólafur Ragnar Grimsson, the former president of Iceland. The Arctic Circle Assembly's major purpose is to promote international cooperation to address the consequences of global warming and environmental degradation of the Arctic.[18] The dynamic problems such as reducing environmentally damaging pollution and toxic chemicals can only be addressed by intense international cooperation. I have learned that the starting point for addressing complex dynamic challenges must begin with our commitment to a mindset of Interdependent Thinking and Acting. But enough about me.

Disposition: Interdependent Thinking and Acting

The CANAM Smart Ports and Harbors Program grant partners are recognized for exceptional work as private and public entities. We are accustomed to addressing complex problems *independently*, on a smaller scale, where aligning objectives, strategies, and resources with numerous partners is not a priority. We are present today because we understand that focusing on one aspect of a complex problem results in modest or mixed results. Yesterday, my dear colleague and friend Marit-Abril introduced you to the capabilities and practices from Cultivating Productive Working Relationships needed to work together effectively as a team across public and private sectors and in diverse heterogeneous communities. The next step for our newly formed CANAM Smart Ports and Harbors Program grants team is to learn and utilize the capabilities and practices for the disposition Interdependent Thinking and Acting.

An unprecedented level of coordination and synchrony of working group actions is needed to achieve a reasonable level of success for the CANAM Smart Ports and Harbors Program grant objectives. We will need to view developing an environment of trust as a precondition before establishing a common understanding of and commitment to the overall grant objectives and the specific goals of each working group. Table 8 outlines the capabilities and practices of Interdependent Thinking and Acting. The first capability is Establish and Maintain an Environment of Trust, the glue that holds any relationship or organization together.

Table 8. Interdependent Thinking and Acting

CAPABILITY: Establish and maintain an environment of trust
PRACTICES:
• Model the *predictable values* of integrity, transparency, and honesty
• Maintain a community with equal status and certainty in ways of working together
• Model *predictable skills* (role competence) for working together
• Maintain an environment of psychological safety
CAPABILITY: Accept a shared understanding of objectives, approaches, and challenges
PRACTICES:
• Foster the acceptance and support of overarching coalition objectives and working group goals
• Create a shared understanding of challenges and agreed-upon approaches to addressing them

- Maintain continuous communication of common objectives and measures of success
- Develop the capacity to look at things from other points of view
- Place aside actions that are incongruent with agreed upon objectives and goals

CAPABILITY: Promote access to resources and coordination across a broader community

PRACTICES:

- Establish opportunities for coalition partners to share data, knowledge, expertise, and wisdom successfully
- Establish practices for coalition partners to coordinate to avoid overlapping efforts and address overlooked activities
- Develop structures to share data, knowledge, resources, and insights of working groups (internal)
- Develop structures to share knowledge, resources, and insights with willing communities (external)

Capability: Establish and Maintain an Environment of Trust

The CAGIS Foundation team members have lived as officers aboard vessels and believe trust is a precondition for leading a crew. Simply put, trust will be present when a crew believes their captain is competent and places their safety first. One of the first questions we ask when interviewing for a maritime command position at Sainte-

Foy Marine, Ltd.: "How do you demonstrate or communicate to a crew that you are trustworthy?" It is the same question all of you must answer if, as a grant team, you hope to work alongside your communities to implement the goals of the grant.

There have been volumes written about what trust is and how we gain or lose it with individuals and within organizations. The *predictable values* we propose are integrity, transparency, and honesty.[19] Integrity is that we act in ways congruent with the promises we have made. Integrity is not a single event where we pronounce that we will have integrity. It is trying, as much as humanly possible, to model, even in brief encounters, that our words and actions are consistent. We openly state that we are capable of mistakes and will fall short, at times, of meeting our agreed upon expectations. Transparency is acknowledging what went wrong and our recommitment to our stated promises. Honesty is simply being truthful and sincere. Finally, transparency and honesty compel us not to seek our own path or put into play an agenda that satisfies goals or outcomes contrary to the work of our team.

It does not imply moral superiority by stating that we should aspire to model the predictable values of integrity, transparency, and honesty. The CAGIS Foundation team commits to the predictable values, acknowledges we will make mistakes, and promises to accept responsibility and make the necessary adjustments. It is helpful to understand that by not overpromising what we can do, we are more likely to be viewed as a colleague with both strengths and limitations. When we make fewer promises with clarity and specificity, we are all more likely to be considered trustworthy.

The second component of trust is *predictable skills* or role competence.[20] The CAGIS team is participating in the CANAM Smart Ports and Harbors Program because each team member is recognized as exceptionally capable and competent in our chosen fields of work. The CANAM Smart Ports and Harbors Program grant team members in this room come from many occupations and perform a set of competencies articulated by our unique profession. The three broad categories for a competent employee at Sainte-Foy Marine are: (a) skillfulness as a mariner, (b) willingness to work effectively as a team member, and (c) openness to learn and improve. An effective professional is expected to consistently exhibit predictable skills.

We invite you to apply your acknowledged professional expertise and acquire or refine a new set of predictable skills. The CANAM Smart Ports and Harbors Program compels us to work together effectively and engage our coastal communities in constructive ways to mediate the effects of rising sea levels. The professional expertise we contribute will be vital to the program's success. However, working together effectively as a team and engaging your respective communities will determine if our expertise makes a difference. The CAGIS Foundation team acknowledges that you might feel a little off-balance and outside your comfort zone when learning a new set of predictable skills. We pledge to develop a professional environment and community that is supportive, a community where we will learn or refine the following CANAM Smart Ports and Harbors predictable skills:

- CANAM norms for team collaboration
- Working agreements (as needed)
- Elements of an effective meeting
- Strategies to support diversity
- Structures for sharing knowledge
- Collect, interpret, and distribute multiple forms of data
- Participate in a network for growth and feedback

Capability: Accept a Shared Understanding of Objectives, Approaches, and Challenges

The mission of the CANAM Smart Ports and Harbors Program was noted when you met yesterday but bears repeating, given that it should be what guides us throughout these five days of leadership training.

Our collective *mission* is to reduce the impact of severe weather events and rising sea levels on our immediate communities by developing and implementing sustainable and adaptable practices. We will collaborate and network to share our knowledge and insights with one another to improve our plans and the outcomes for our communities.

This mission is what brings us together, and the dispositions the CAGIS Foundation team presents across these five days at sea will assist our teams in successfully meeting the following four objectives:

- Engage communities
- Build capacity
- Create useable case studies
- Develop a coastal community framework and a practical guide

Ultimately, model solutions and innovations developed by the CANAM Smart Ports and Harbors Program grant awardees will be available to any interested coastal village, town, or city.

Objective One: Engage Communities

The objectives and approaches of the CANAM Smart Ports and Harbors Program require the engagement of the coastal zone communities as fundamental to the success of the grant. Typically, involvement of a broader community occurs after grant activities have concluded, and this has frequently led to the perception that elite outsiders without local knowledge or understanding want to impose their solutions on the unenlightened. Our work must engage communities before and during our grant activities. Our work must be guided by the priorities and values of those being impacted in coastal communities. Members of the three coastal zone communities are needed as the grant begins to *collect data* and assist with *implementing any actions* that are recommended.

The CANAM Smart Ports and Harbors Program grant selected North American coastal zone areas in the Pacific Ocean, the Atlantic Ocean, and the Gulf of Mexico. The knowledge base about how sea level rise affects an entire coastal zone community remains extremely limited, including the impact on shipping, resource development, recreation, fisheries, and tourism. The knowledge base about sea level rise regional variability is extremely limited. Mechanisms for establishing detailed baseline data and strategies for collecting information in the future are urgently needed.

Objective Two: Build Capacity

Coastal zone needs assessments are necessary to inform decision-making and will depend upon long-term monitoring of ocean tides, currents, temperature, and salinity. The documentation of observed migration and behavior of marine mammals and seabirds will also be needed. A vessel of opportunity (VOO) program will recruit 150 interested community members in each coastal zone community. Similar VOO programs for whale migration and oil spill response have been enormously successful and expand exponentially the information that can be collected.[21] It also involves those who can craft and implement strategies for their own communities.

Objective Three: Create Useable Case Studies

The CANAM Smart Ports and Harbors Program grant will focus on ways to reduce coastal vulnerability while identifying ways to increase adaptability for the three coastal zone communities involved in the grant. Solutions such as levees and seawalls are impractical in some settings, while land use changes in other settings might not be politically palatable. If possible, the case studies will provide potential solutions that are ecologically sustainable and economically affordable for each specific coastal zone community.

The case studies will incorporate promising approaches that are viable and provide possible new strategies that are cost-effective. For example, elevating structures and maintaining or enhancing existing land buffers have proven helpful when specific conditions are met. The case studies will include Traditional Ecological Knowledge (TEK).

Objective Four: Develop a Coastal Community Framework and a Practical Guide

The CANAM Smart Ports and Harbors Program will develop a framework and practical guide for responding to sea level rise. The technical knowledge acquired during the grant and the data collection systems that inform our decision-making will be made available to others. The strategies and approaches for productively engaging a coastal community as partners will be developed and shared. The guide will provide approaches to address the environmental, social-emotional, economic, political, and legal implications for proactively responding to sea level rise.

The CANAM Smart Ports and Harbors Program grant has funds for the three coastal zone communities to begin implementing tangible short-term strategies identified in the specific community case study. The grant funding organizations will establish a process for evaluating and funding the implementation plan for Port of Pascagoula and the Harbors of Pascagoula and Biloxi, Mississippi; the Port of Vancouver and Steveston Harbour on the Fraser River and Nanaimo Harbour on Vancouver Island; and the Port of Halifax and the Harbours of Halifax and Lunenburg, Nova Scotia.

The three coastal zone communities have over thirty cooperating agencies addressing numerous working group goals. The four objectives are designed to provide enough guidance and focus for all working group goals and activities while allowing enough flexibility to address the circumstances in three quite different coastal zone communities. We ask that you commit to aligning working group goals with the four objectives and to the CANAM Smart Ports and Harbors Program communication plan designed for sharing data, findings, and insights.

There are two important considerations for Interdependent Thinking and Acting, especially when teams are organizationally, culturally, and demographically diverse. First, the capacity to look at things from other points of view before asserting or commenting is a thoughtful default position. Second, placing aside actions that are incongruent with the agreed-upon objectives and the specific working group goals is essential. It is expected that cooperating agencies will have organizational objectives and goals that are aligned with the CANAM Smart Ports and Harbors Program. Those objectives and goals not aligned with the CANAM Smart Ports and Harbors Program will need to be addressed through venues other than this grant.

Capability: Promote Access to Resources and Coordination Across a Broader Community

The CANAM Smart Ports and Harbors Program grant has opportunities and convenings for climate scientists to share data and advance research activity as it pertains to sea level rise in the three coastal community zones. There are several climate scientists participating in the training aboard the R/V *Smart Ports* here today. They are present to support the implications of climate science research, specifically sea level rise, and how it might translate into informing the four grant objectives. The five days of leadership training will, hopefully, bridge the small chasm that often exists between what we know and how our knowledge translates into tangible actions. The four grant objectives — engage communities, build capacity, create useable case studies, and develop a coastal community framework and a practical guide — are designed to positively influence the adaptations and adjustments coastal community zones will need to make for their long-term survival.

Structured Opportunities for Coalition Partners to Share Knowledge and Expertise

The expertise in this room is extraordinary. It will benefit the CANAM Smart Ports and Harbors Program team only if it advances our collective understanding of the implications of sea level rise. The practices and structures that will be put in place are intended to allow each of you to make contributions informed by your area of expertise. This will require cooperation, collaboration, and interdependence. Thinking and acting interdependently, as noted earlier, begins when we develop relational trust with one another.

The communication structures that will be put in place will be coordinated by the CANAM Smart Ports and Harbors Program event staff. A survey will be administered to determine preferred scheduled synchronous opportunities and preferred platforms for asynchronous opportunities to share information. The intent of the survey is to arrange schedules that respect your valuable time and utilize the methods that your team currently uses for internal and external communication. We will schedule two face-to-face convenings each year with all three coastal zone teams and arrange multiple opportunities for within and between team exchanges. The CAGIS Foundation team appreciates that time is a precious resource and understands that if it is not coordinated and protected on a calendar, information sharing is less likely to happen.

We asked each participant here today to prepare a brief one-page document that states several key professional areas of focus and the personal interests that are integral to how others might connect with you. The participant list that is provided contains an area to write a brief note about each team member in the room. Time will be provided each day to get to know the wonderful colleagues who, like you, are committed to the success of the CANAM Smart Ports and Harbors Program grant.

Practices will be established to carefully coordinate activities to avoid overlapping efforts and to address overlooked activities as described in all the grant work plans. The idea of coordinating activities requires interdependent thinking about the interplay between the activities of each team. Inviting all participants to be vigilant about overlooked activities requires a level of trust and transparency so individuals might speak up about their observations or concerns. The CANAM Smart Ports and Harbors Program team will need to be information-enabled and evidence-based to effectively coordinate efforts and determine overlooked activities. Ultimately, data collection systems, information utilization, and protocols will be needed to make decisions about the impact of the grant. Fortunately, the disposition Gathering Information for Improvement and Innovation will be our next topic.

Chapter Three:
Questions to Engage Your Thinking and for Discussion or Dialogue with Colleagues

The first capability of Interdependent Thinking and Acting is to Establish and Maintain an Environment of Trust, noted as the glue that holds any relationship or organization together. Jean-Philippe states that developing an environment of trust is a precondition before establishing a collective understanding of, and commitment to, the overall grant objectives and the specific goals of each working group.

1. How would you describe the relationship between the capability of Establish and Maintain an Environment of Trust and the disposition of Interdependent Thinking and Acting?

2. How and why is an environment of trust a precondition to successfully establishing common grant objectives and goals?

3. From your experiences and perspective, how does Establish and Maintain an Environment of Trust serve as "the glue that holds any relationship or organization together"?

Jean-Philippe tells the grantees that one of the first interview questions he asks is for a maritime command position at Sainte-Foy Marine, Ltd., is "How do you demonstrate or communicate to a crew that you are trustworthy?"

4. How would you answer that question in relation to those you supervise or colleagues/team members? In other words, how do you demonstrate or communicate to others that you are trustworthy?

The CAGIS Foundation team proposes integrity, transparency, and honesty as the *predictable values* needed to develop and maintain trust.

5. Are there other predictable values that you believe are needed to develop and maintain trust within an organization?

6. Please refer to Appendix B for an opportunity to actively participate as a team member of the Nova Scotia Coastal Climate Collaborative. The collaborative represents the Port of Halifax, Nova Scotia, and the Harbours of Halifax and Lunenburg, Nova Scotia. The team is deliberating over how to utilize the capabilities and practices from the disposition Interdependent Thinking and Acting.

Chapter Four

DAY THREE—Gathering Information for Improvement and Innovation, Sidney to Friday Harbor

Erika Knudsen Presents

My name is Erika Knudsen, and I lived most of my early years in Tórshavn, the capital of the Faroe Islands. The Faroe Islands are part of the Kingdom of Denmark and are 1,125 kilometers, or 700 miles, from the Danish coast in the North Atlantic Ocean. My family members were commercial fishers until we purchased a salmon farming operation. I attended the University of Copenhagen and earned a doctorate in cognitive science. I eventually was a professor at the University of Copenhagen. Because of my academic background, the CAGIS Foundation team asked me to research and design the leadership framework we are using today.

    I faced the challenges of being a minority in Tórshavn, a community with a population of primarily Nordic heritage where not everyone welcomed a biracial girl. My Danish had a slight accent because Faroese word pronunciation is like Norwegian. There were, of course, some Danish elites at the University of Copenhagen who looked down upon me because of my biracial heritage and slight accent. It was a defining reason I turned to cognitive science to study strategies to change behaviors and, hopefully, the beliefs that form misconceptions that lead to prejudice and racism.

People share more in their common humanity than the physical and verbal differences of race and language. When I shared this information with Marit-Abril, Nora, Jean-Philippe, and Lincoln, the team understood why I had personal and professional insights that influenced my development of the *Respectful & Productive Relationships* program. This program that proactively addresses the male-dominated maritime culture and the possibility of sexist behavior.

The retirement I anticipated as an emeritus professor was short-lived. My life partner, Monique, and I spend summers in Tórshavn with my delightful parents, Aksel and Kosum Knudsen. I was residing in Tórshavn when Marit-Abril, Lincoln, Nora, and Jean-Philippe invited me to be part of this remarkable team and professional opportunity. I mention my summer residence in the Faroe Islands because all the team members who are hosting you today return to the wonderful maritime environments often that feed our souls. And it is our deeply held belief that we should take responsibility for the challenges we face today to ensure future generations have the opportunities that sustain us economically, culturally, and environmentally.

I participated in numerous large-scale research and program evaluation projects while at the University of Copenhagen. The lessons I learned about striving to make evidence-based decisions shaped my understanding of the ways in which data, in its many forms, might be utilized. I feel compelled to share a few of the lessons I have learned over two decades of designing viable and usable program evaluations. The terminology we use to describe the information collected, the routines we establish for sharing data, and the data displays should all match the intended audience.

Disposition: Gathering Information for Improvement and Innovation

We are gathered aboard the RV *Smart Ports* to learn leadership skills that will assist us in our work with the CANAM Smart Ports and Harbors Program. This is an amazing opportunity for us to reduce the impact of severe weather events and rising sea levels on our immediate communities. The disposition of *Gathering Information for Improvement and Innovation* is critical to our success in reaching the goals and objectives of the CANAM Smart Ports and Harbors Program. Table 9 notes the three capabilities associated with the disposition of *Gathering Information for Improvement and Innovation*: systematically gathering and reporting quantitative and qualitative data, using data to inform decisions and actions, and developing an environment of open-minded inquiry for continuous improvement. We will need to be able to understand and explain the information we collect. More importantly, if we want to effect change, we will need to use data to inform decisions and engage our constituencies to work collaboratively with valid and reliable information. None of these are easy tasks.

Table 9. Disposition: Gathering Information for Improvement and Innovation

CAPABILITY: Systematically gather and report quantitative and qualitative data (what)
PRACTICES:
• Seek multiple and diverse forms of data to assess inputs, outputs, outcomes, and impact
• Prioritize data sets to support coalition objectives and working group goals
• Establish routines for sharing and using prioritized quantitative and qualitative data
• Report consistently on a short list of indicators

CAPABILITY: Use data to inform decisions and actions (how)
PRACTICES:
• Establish a culture of evidence-based decision-making
• Establish routines and protocols for analyzing and interpreting data
• Include multiple perspectives and diverse perspectives when interpreting data and using it to inform decision-making
• Identify additional data sources to further inform decision-making
• Establish common language for data fluency, interpretation, and analyses
CAPABILITY: Develop an environment of open-minded inquiry for continuous improvement
PRACTICES:
• Work collaboratively in an environment of openness and transparency
• Seek multiple perspectives and points of view
• Place aside initial assumptions when examining data
• Establish a shared sense of responsibility for using data to achieve common goals

> - Develop an environment of inquiry to foster insights and discovery

Capability: Systematically Gather and Report Quantitative and Qualitative Data

Quantitative data include information that utilizes numbers, measurements, descriptive and inferential statistics. Making inferences with quantitative data is considered more powerful when validity and reliability are utilized. Quantitative data can be generalizable but lacks the detail and nuanced description inherent in qualitative data.

Qualitative data can take many forms, such as interviews, questionnaires and surveys, observations, documents, records, focus groups, and in certain situations, oral histories. We can better understand and make sense of a situation by recording specific details and describing the context through the mentioned forms. Qualitative data are not typically generalizable but contain the detail and description not inherent in quantitative data.

The idea that we must master data collection and all the intricate methods used to interpret data is unrealistic. A team of data geeks like myself, representing each coastal zone involved in the grant, is developing the systems and methods for data collection and reporting all project information. Each team has been provided the data plan for your respective coastal zone to share with the other teams present today. Gathering information can be overwhelming and even misleading without an understanding of what is being collected, how it is managed, and a sound rationale for interpreting the data. A place to begin creating our mutual understanding of data is to describe the forms of information we will be collecting.

Two important considerations I learned while doing program evaluations are 1) the complexity of data conversations and displays must match the intended audience, and 2) quantitative data and qualitative data are most powerful when both are used to inform decision-making. For example, "big data analytics" utilizes the power of computer programming to analyze large sample sizes of both quantitative and qualitative data and, when designed effectively, can provide predictive models that assist researchers in understanding possible future outcomes.[22]

It is unlikely that detailed analyses performed by the scientists at each of the locations will be shared routinely. With your guidance and feedback, the data dashboards we will create will report consistently on a short list of indicators that all three project locations can use with their respective constituencies. The CAGIS Foundation team and each of your respective teams will need to engage in thoughtful dialogue around the types of data collection and data dashboard questions noted in Table 10.

Table 10. Questions to Consider in Making Decisions Regarding Data Collection and Dashboard Displays

Why are you collecting data? (What questions are you trying to answer? What types of decisions are you trying to inform? What are you trying to improve and why?)
Which sites or areas are designated for data collection?
What resources (e.g., time, money, expertise) are needed?
Who will collect the data?
What specific data needs to be collected?
How frequently will the data be collected?
How will you assess the reliability, validity, and meaningfulness of findings?

How will the data and findings be used to make program improvements and inform decision-making?
How will you engage your communities with data in helpful and meaningful ways?
Which indicators should appear on a data dashboard for all teams to access and share externally? Why?
What technical data will be shared by scientists and engineers internally?

The team representing the Port of Vancouver and the team representing the Port of Halifax are utilizing Data Carpentry's fundamental data literacy training modules with the assistance of Compute Canada. Both organizations subscribe to assisting individuals in utilizing data in accessible and meaningful ways. This is especially important since a common goal is engaging communities with information that is easy to access and free of jargon and acronyms. Data Carpentry and Compute Canada have a code of conduct that is consistent with the values of all partnering organizations.

Routines for Sharing Data

An important task for today is to establish and commit to a predictable cycle of routines for information sharing that are clearly understood. I learned that program evaluations were enhanced by developing a detailed plan for sharing and releasing data. This might sound like a simple proposition; however, data sharing is made complex because of the number of participating organizations, the various types of data collected, and the different schedules and expectations for engaging constituent groups.

Your web-based team folder has a spreadsheet that multiple users can access, and it contains the fields in Table 11, Template for a Common Data Calendar. We invite your team to start the process of populating the spreadsheet. Of course, this is just the beginning, and many other participants not here today will need to be consulted. You are encouraged to utilize Table 4, Sample Working Agreements, and Table 5, Team Member Meeting Roles, before you begin. These two handouts that you received on your first day support efficient and effective team collaboration.

Table 11. Template for a Common Data Calendar

Month	Organization and Contact Person	Data Collected	When will Data be Submitted/ Uploaded	When will Data be Presented
Ongoing	Fisheries and Oceans Canada Halifax (J. Bellevue) Vancouver (H. Chan)	GPS location, date, and time for tides, currents, temperature, and salinity	Monthly (due the third day of following month)	Undecided currently

Work Collaboratively in an Environment of Openness and Transparency

It is especially critical that we freely share the collected data to achieve the goal of being evidence-based. The memorandum of understanding (MOU) we agreed to outlines the ethical and transparent use of all the information we gather. The MOU clearly articulates how data will be collected, stored, protected, retained, analyzed, and reported. What is less clear is how we might engage communities with information that is accessible, jargon-free, understandable, and useful. The approaches we decide to utilize, in the form of discussion protocols and processes for dialogue, will help guide deliberations about what options are available for responding to increasingly severe weather events and rising sea levels.

We will be engaging and presenting information to our constituencies in small groups and public forums. There is certainly skepticism of science and denial of the impact of global climate change and rising sea levels. Our approach to using data to guide decision-making must be unwavering. The credibility we earn will rest squarely on being open and transparent about the information that is collected and analyzed.

I learned a critical lesson doing fieldwork as a researcher and program evaluator. The approach used to engage constituents and community groups can be perceived negatively and even with hostility. It is essential to communicate and engage those not involved directly in work as partners in data collection and as equals in the decision-making process. If our approach is not inclusive, the feedback received might show that we are perceived as arrogant and elitist, dismissive of the less formally well-educated or those individuals and groups perceived as culturally less sophisticated. The information and strategies introduced during the first two days by Marit-Abril and Jean-Philippe will increase the odds that we can develop credible relationships with the communities we hope to assist.

Discussion Protocols and Processes for Dialogue

It is important to make the distinction between the responsibilities of the scientific community and the responsibilities of the participants present here today. The technical analyses and interpretation of data will be conducted by scientists representing each of the coastal zone teams. Our mission as leadership teams is to identify data that we will share and report in a user-friendly format and engage organizations and communities. *How* to engage organizations and communities with information in helpful and meaningful ways requires skillful facilitation and strategies to support successful individual and group interactions. Two such approaches, dialogue and discussion, were introduced by Marit-Abril two days ago.

Discussion is a convergent process used to propose solutions, prioritize, identify potential decisions, and select a course of action. Using discussion protocols with questions and meeting structures will lead to more successful outcomes. For example, the Elements of an Effective Meeting, as described in Table 6, are useful for creating the environment for an efficient and effective discussion. We will be developing several discussion protocols with questions sequenced from descriptive to analytical.

Dialogue is a divergent and nonjudgmental process that explores choices or creates a commonly shared understanding. It does not conclude with a decision. Effective open-ended questioning strategies are useful during a dialogue because they sustain the thinking of team members. The use of tentative languages such as the word *might* and the use of plural forms such as the word *ways* supports deeper thinking about the information that is presented. For example, a facilitator would state: What *might* be other *ways* to interpret the information that was presented this afternoon?

Strategies for using discussion and dialogue, as well as sample discussion protocols and dialogue strategies, will be the focus of team time this afternoon. The input provided by all three teams later today, and feedback suggested for refining the first drafts, will be posted in the shared file. It is anticipated that facilitation resources will be developed with frequent web-based learning opportunities for team members present today.

Capability: Use Data to Inform Decisions and Actions

An excellent example of beginning the process of building a partnership with a shared sense of responsibility for using data in each of the three coastal zones is the Vessel of Opportunity (VOO) program. Recruitment has started by enlisting 150 interested working vessel owners in each coastal zone community represented here today. The CANAM Smart Ports and Harbors Program grant has purchased equipment for collecting real-time information about long-term monitoring of ocean tides, currents, temperature, and salinity. The documentation of observed migration and behavior of marine mammals and seabirds will also be collected. Seeking assistance with data collection is about being open and transparent within communities that will need to eventually implement strategies. In some cases, it will require difficult financial and political decisions. Data collected by community members will provide credibility for the decision-making process.

We appreciate that the teams from the Port of Pascagoula and the Harbors of Pascagoula and Biloxi, Mississippi; the Port of Vancouver and Steveston Harbour on the Fraser River and Nanaimo Harbour in British Columbia; and the Port of Halifax and the Harbours of Halifax and Lunenburg, Nova Scotia, are already recruiting vessel owners with a great deal of success. It is anticipated that as many as 450 vessels will be participating in data collection. VOO programs for whale migration and oil spill response have been enormously successful and have exponentially expanded the information that can be collected for scientists to interpret changes in the maritime environment.

The information that will be collected by participating Vessels of Opportunity is displayed on the monitors around this meeting area. It is real-time information that is being collected for ocean tides, currents, temperature, and salinity by the RV *Smart Ports*.

Seek Multiple Perspectives and Points of View

There are residents in the participating coastal communities who possess deep knowledge and insights about their immediate environment. Indigenous people have passed on detailed knowledge through generations of direct experience that is often an untapped resource for understanding changes in climate patterns. Traditional Ecological Knowledge (TEK) is a vital source of knowledge that will hopefully be shared and considered as valuable as any source of information that is collected. Lincoln Angiak, a valued team member and presenter on the final day of the voyage, has been instrumental in formulating our approach to seeking local and Indigenous knowledge.

Capability: Develop an Environment of Open-minded Inquiry for Continuous Improvement

An environment of open-minded inquiry begins with transparency about the availability of data and the intentions for its use. Decisions about the implications of the data require being receptive to multiple viewpoints and recognizing that our assumptions are not always accurate and that we all are susceptible to confirmation bias. It is common to seek information that affirms what we believe to be true, and it is a contributing factor to making flawed decisions. This will be especially important when diverse coastal communities are invited to participate in meetings, and challenges will need to be addressed.

Temporarily placing aside assumptions and not asserting a point of view establishes that all members have equal status within the group. This is realized by simply listening to others. A useful reminder for all group members is to inquire about the thoughts and opinions of others before asserting their own views or opinions. It is healthy and common to disagree with ideas and opinions that are placed before the group. A reminder for maintaining productive professional relationships is to remember to disagree with ideas and not with people.

The CANAM Norms were developed to reinforce the notion that unless respectful relationships and processes are in place, the solutions that will assist coastal communities threatened by the effects of climate change are far less likely to happen. Marit-Abril, Nora, Jean-Philippe, Lincoln, and I firmly believe that some of our professional situations would have been more productive if we had 1) listened to understand, 2) acknowledged equal status, 3) modeled being transparent and open, and 4) remembered to disagree with ideas and not with people. We invite you to utilize any of our collective hard-earned wisdom with the hope that it might benefit your working professional relationships.

Chapter Four:
Questions to Engage Your Thinking and for Discussion or Dialogue with Colleagues

The three capabilities associated with the disposition of Gathering Information for Improvement and Innovation are systematically gathering and reporting quantitative and qualitative data, using data to inform decisions and actions, and developing an environment of open-minded inquiry for continuous improvement.

1. Which of these capabilities do you see as being the most difficult for an organization? Why?

2. What are examples you have observed or experienced firsthand as part of an organization where data were extensively used to inform decisions and actions? How did the organization in your example differ from those organizations that do not use data to inform decisions and actions?

Erika Knudsen describes a lesson learned while doing fieldwork as a researcher and program evaluator. She noted that constituents and community groups are not always receptive to data collected and analyzed by those outside the community and may even view findings negatively or with hostility.

3. What strategies, behaviors, and approaches (before data collection, during data collection, and in reporting findings) might be used to minimize the chances of a community reacting negatively or with hostility?

4. How can other dispositions and capabilities discussed in previous chapters be used by the CANAM Smart Ports and Harbors Program teams to develop credible relationships

with their communities such that there is an environment of open-minded inquiry developed between grant teams and their respective communities?

Chapter Five

DAY FOUR—Seeking Support and Feedback that Fosters Growth, Friday Harbor to La Conner Harbor

Nora Jensen Presents

I am Nora Jensen, born in Oudenaarde, Belgium, on the River Scheldt in the Flemish province of East Flanders. I lived aboard the *St. Walburga,* which my parents would lease through a broker for short-term payloads and at times to a company for an extended lease. The *St. Walburga,* like most inland waterway barges, had a small crane for freight, and it was used to load and unload the family compact automobile that was stored on deck. St. Walburga is the special patroness of seafarers, and she is invoked by sailors for safety in storms.[23] The Belgium canal and river system is part of the Inland Waterway Transport (IWT) that provides shipping of international freight through an extensive transportation corridor vital to many European countries.

The River Scheldt flows through Antwerp, the second-largest port in Europe, with direct access to the North Sea. I could see the Antwerp Maritime Academy from the deck of the *St. Walburga*, where the River Scheldt makes a 90-degree turn west and heads to the North Sea. I lived aboard the *St. Walburga* until I attended a residential high school in Antwerp and was one of the first women to enroll in the Antwerp Maritime Academy. I excelled academically and technically because of the experiences and responsibilities I had aboard the *St. Walburga.* It was both exciting and challenging to be one of the first women to enter an academy that is male-oriented and a profession that is male-dominated. Many classmates and instructors were skeptical of a woman excelling in a world where the female pronoun *she* refers more often to the ship than to its captain.

Upon graduation, Maersk Line A/S, an international container shipping company based in Copenhagen, hired me. I was a chief mate aboard the *Aotea Maersk,* a large container ship registered and sailed under the flag of Denmark. Morten Pedersen, the chief operating officer of Maersk Line A/S, took the lead in integrating women into the command structure aboard company ships.[24] He did two *proactive* things to enhance my success as one of the first female officers aboard a Maersk Line ship. First, Pedersen assigned a female second mate aboard the *Aotea Maersk,* so the second and third in command of the ship were women. He had the forethought to assign us under the command of a popular and receptive captain. Master Aksel Madsen was trained in *Respectful & Productive Relationships*, a program developed by Erika Knudsen, your presenter, yesterday. The *Respectful & Productive Relationships* program proactively addressed the male-dominated maritime culture and the possibility of sexist behavior directed at the two new officers aboard the *Aotea Maersk.*

The experiences I had as a cadet and as a crew member affirmed the need to be proactive about how we treat one another regardless of race, gender, national identity, sexual orientation. I learned that careful planning and anticipating reactions are vital to success, rather than being reactive when altering the status quo. As the first woman in a command position aboard a vessel in the company's history, careful planning helped me, and it also helped the crew in an uncommon situation that is now more commonplace, thankfully.

Master Aksel Madsen communicated clear and unambiguous expectations for how the crew could respectfully interact without using biased, inflammatory, or inappropriate gestures or language. A new world was challenging the province of male mariners. The command structure aboard ships had been in place for centuries, with a few notable exceptions. The planning, the support, and the training happened before I went aboard the *Aotea Maersk* with a female colleague. Maersk Line A/S wanted all crew members to have the opportunity to be successful.

I worked my way up to master and commanded several large container ships for Maersk Line A/S before being selected as the executive director of safety and training. In that position, I worked with chief mates who were responsible for the safety and security of their ships. I encouraged and mentored the chief mates who were considered promising and ready for selection as a ship's master. A remarkable program at Port Revel in the French Alps that trained maritime pilots and ship officers to learn maneuvers on small-scaled, carefully engineered model ships influenced my beliefs about support and feedback greatly.[25] These two experiences changed my career trajectory and were the genesis of the SEE for SEAfarers Mentoring Model. (The acronym SEE is the feedback sequence of supporting, expecting, encouraging.)

I met my business partner, Jean-Philippe Gagnon, who presented to you two days ago at a maritime conference. Together, we positioned the company he had founded, Sainte-Foy Marine, Ltd., as a source of income and a beacon for social change. I am convinced that making money and influencing social change do not have to be diametrically opposing goals. For example, we support access to the maritime industry for first-generation students, many of whom are women and Indigenous people, and often female and First Nation tribal members.

Disposition: Seeking Support and Feedback that Fosters Growth

The material we will learn, examine, and explore today takes a departure from the past three days. *Inter*personal skills and *inter*dependent actions, the focus of presentations on day one and day two, rely heavily on the strategies we summon for interacting with individuals and groups. Gathering qualitative and quantitative data, the focus of day three, requires specific content knowledge and the facilitation skills for using information with colleagues, community members, and organizations.

The focus today is on *ourselves as leaders* or the *intra*personal dimension of leadership. It is the unavoidable intersection of developing leadership capacities as a professional while drawing upon the personal characteristics of honesty, humility, and integrity. The professional self is influenced by our personal beliefs, values, and willingness to seek support and feedback. On many levels, our professional and personal identities are ultimately inseparable from one another. The growth we hope to experience as we learn to lead others is contingent on being self-aware and having self-knowledge about our inclinations, strengths, and weaknesses. Personal and professional growth is dependent upon our willingness to be honest with ourselves.

Over the past fifteen years, I learned a few significant lessons while teaching *Respectful & Productive Relationships*, implementing the SEE for SEAfarers Mentoring Model, and modeling the Descriptive Feedback Protocol. One lesson I learned: The professionals who benefited the most were humble enough to recognize that a willingness to accept constructive feedback accelerated their acquisition of professional expertise. Humility is not the absence of a strong sense of self. It is the ability to recognize our own strengths and weaknesses. This self-knowledge benefits the individual and those with whom we work.

The mariners who learned a tricky maneuver quickly, such as operating a vessel in a difficult and stressful situation, were receptive to immediate constructive feedback. They exhibited a willingness to adjust their current knowledge base and skill set to act efficiently and with precision. It was through guidance and persistence that learning new information was accelerated and through ongoing support that greater job satisfaction was reported. It is the intention of the CAGIS Foundation team to create the conditions needed so that the disposition of *Seeking Support and Feedback that Fosters Growth* becomes attainable for each participant here today. Table 12 notes the capabilities and respective practices associated with this disposition.

Table 12. Disposition: Seeking Support and Feedback that Fosters Growth

CAPABILITY: Develop Self-knowledge and Self-awareness (myself)
PRACTICES:
• Know one's strengths
• Know one's weaknesses
• Understand one's inclinations
• Recognize personal growth and professional excellence are interconnected
• Maintain a sense of humility
CAPABILITY: Create a Professional System for Support and Feedback (colleagues)
PRACTICES:
• Establish norms of interaction that provide a supportive environment for honest reflection

- Develop trusting and supportive relationships that are reciprocal
- Be intentional in seeking support from trusted colleagues
- Seek constructive feedback from others
- Engage in honest collegial dialogue, exchange of ideas, and honest debate over issues

Capability: Develop Self-knowledge and Self-awareness

There is a multitude of schema describing the *self* that has overlapping definitions and similar qualities that can confuse and distort an understanding of ourselves. Self-knowledge and external self-awareness are the two areas of the self that we selected because both ideas are particularly helpful for improving our leadership role in the workplace.[26] A challenge in learning about the *intra*-personal dimension of leadership is that approaches tend toward one of two extremes: the approach either focuses on surface-level self-help strategies that are superficial, or the approach focuses on the opposite extreme of a deep dive into examining the self and entering a world too complex to describe. We all have the capacity to learn about ourselves, and when we do, it is usually hard-earned through the successes and failures of experience in our work and private lives.

For our purposes, self-knowledge is understanding the mental models and values that inform our thinking and behavior in the workplace. It is knowing one's strengths and weaknesses, one's beliefs and biases, and the values that motivate one's decisions. Humility is a key component of utilizing self-knowledge. Humility allows us to understand ourselves, acknowledge our blind spots, and assume responsibility for our actions. The CAGIS Foundation team has used several personality inventories over the past several years that have been a catalyst for gaining self-knowledge. The inventories have also helped me appreciate how team members might interact with one another.

It is through external self-awareness, comparing one's outward behavior to internal mental models or shared values, that we develop the capacity for introspection. External self-awareness is necessary for viewing the impact of our behavior on others and, hopefully, making needed adjustments. It allows leaders to gain insight into how they might be perceived. It is through interacting with others that our blind spots are revealed. External self-awareness affords us the opportunity to consider whether the actions we take are congruent with our espoused beliefs. When we step back and take stock, we can discover areas for personal and professional growth. Ultimately, we will become better people and more effective leaders through external self-awareness.

There will always be tension between the idiocentric, focusing on our interests, and the allocentric, focusing on the needs of the greater community. We will never resolve the tension between asserting what will advance our professional standing with considering how we might advance the greater good. A competitive environment and a cooperative environment exist simultaneously. The teams in this room competed for a grant award with other entities and, by doing so, advanced the interests of their respective organizations—the idiocentric impulse. The diverse group present today will be well served if we choose to expand our shared knowledge and increase the competencies of the group to benefit our communities—the allocentric impulse.

Some of us are inclined to be competitive and enjoy the idea that the highest placement or rank at work or play is the best possible outcome. Others among us who regard cooperation and collaboration as the highest calling, and helping others is an end in and of itself. Of course, most of us fall somewhere on the competitive/collaborative continuum, and it is essential for leaders to know and understand their inclination in this area. We are well served by recognizing when and when not to advance the competitive impulse because it can overshadow collaborative effort. Conversely, if not understood, the cooperative and collaborative impulse can lead to inaction and empathy fatigue.

The CAGIS Foundation team utilizes a Descriptive Feedback Protocol when teaching a sea captain to dock a ship. There are numerous maneuvers that can dock a vessel safely. The question is: Which specific maneuver in this situation is the better choice considering the effects of wind, tide, current, and water displacement? This question is analogous to understanding the need to balance the competitive impulse with the cooperative spirit. The question: Given the specific circumstances, does competition or cooperation assist us with attaining the desired outcome? The CAGIS Foundation team would like you to extend this type of thinking even further. The five CAGIS *Dispositions of Leadership* and the corresponding practices are utilized well when considering the thinking and actions best suited to a specific context.

Capability: Create a Professional System for Support and Feedback

Marit-Abril, Erika, Jean-Philippe, Lincoln, and I are committed to supporting one another and being receptive to constructive feedback for professional growth. We learned important lessons about how to structure a productive professional relationship and why it is important. It was through developing the SEE for SEAfarers Mentoring Model and observing the benefits of support and feedback that we decided, as a team, to apply the best of what we learned in our own professional situations.

Jean-Philippe and I also recognized through efforts to retain our valued employees at Sainte-Foy Marine that a supportive network of peers resulted in early career officers acquiring skills at an accelerated rate with fewer mishaps. These officers learned to manage difficult situations with precision, and many reported greater job satisfaction because of supportive colleagues. It is our intention to create these conditions within the CANAM network.

The nature of our collegial network will focus initially on the strategies and practices from the CAGIS *Dispositions of Leadership*. The CAGIS Foundation team learned that a collegial relationship for support and feedback needs to be voluntary, trust-based, constructive (do no harm), nonjudgmental, and utilize the strategies for effective interpersonal communication. The suggested configuration for each team is three or four members from various organizations.

Marit-Abril requested that one of the first tasks for this convening should be to collect detailed professional information from all participants aboard the RV *Smart Ports*. We have allocated time for *home group* teams to form, and we anticipate that you all are receptive to being on a team as described in the pre-conference materials. Please use the recording sheet to identify potential team members with similar roles or professional circumstances in their respective organizations. One compelling reason for forming these networks across different grant teams is so each member can identify structures and skills for seeking support and feedback from other team members.

A partial list of topics introduced this week is provided in Table 13. We encourage each member of the newly formed team to identify the topics of interest that might increase individual or team/group effectiveness in your organization. The seven topics are listed deliberately in a sequence that first provides a foundation for team development before engaging in more challenging ideas or topics.

Table 13. The Seven Topics for Team Collaboration Time

Sequential Topics for Team Time	Rank Order of Importance to You
CANAM Norms for Team Collaboration	
Sample Working Agreements	
Establish and Maintain an Environment of Trust	
Team Member Meeting Roles	
Elements of an Effective Meeting	
Discussion and Dialogue	
Strategies to Support Diversity	

Collegial Dialogue and Constructive Feedback

The professional dialogue we encourage for the newly formed teams is based upon mentoring early career mariners and using the Descriptive Feedback Protocol over the past seven years. The structure and process are outlined in Table 14, the CANAM Team Protocol. We invite you to consider using it. The experiences implementing elements of this protocol taught the CAGIS Foundation team numerous lessons, which we will share. The protocol will have three components: 1) listening and asking questions, 2) providing solicited feedback, and 3) structuring the conversation. Hopefully, a clear process and a defined structure will guide the conversation and make it productive, effective, and an efficient use of time.

The CAGIS Foundation team modeled a specific communication pattern while providing feedback to experienced command staff learning a difficult maneuver. The pattern: listen carefully; paraphrase; ask clarifying or probing questions if more information is needed *before* responding, making assumptions, or drawing conclusions. A person's voice, tone, and body language communicate being an attentive listener as much as the words that are spoken. An effective communication pattern increases the odds of developing a respectful professional relationship.

The CAGIS team noticed while training command staff that it is easy to slip into familiar ways of talking and deviate from the CANAM Team Protocol communication pattern. It is challenging to learn an unfamiliar communication pattern. You might slip into a back-and-forth conversation without pausing or paraphrasing.[27] A team member might start giving unsolicited advice or even stray from the intended topic. It is helpful to place aside these tendencies temporarily and discover the power of effective listening and the benefits of constructive feedback. Please be kind to yourselves as you learn a new communication pattern.

It takes practice and self-discipline to learn how to provide useful and constructive feedback. Some organizational cultures allow and even encourage individuals to make tart comments, sarcastic retorts, and judgmental statements as a way of communicating. In this type of culture, listening is devalued when being assertive, aggressive, and competing for the communication space is up for grabs. This undisciplined communication is often about the speaker and distracts from being an effective listener.

We suggest that feedback is for the benefit of a colleague and occurs in a specific setting with an agreed-upon protocol. *Feedback* is effective when it is *specific, manageable, factual,* and focuses on behaviors that are *alterable*.[28] A person will more likely respond positively to specific rather than vague information. The amount of information provided must be manageable; otherwise, it can overwhelm the recipient. Feedback needs to be fact-based. Stating opinions and giving advice should be avoided in a collegial dialogue. Finally, feedback is based on alterable characteristics or behaviors within a person's control.

The final component of the CANAM Team Protocol is the structure of the conversation. It is suggested that groups of three or four are the ideal group size and allow enough time for all members to participate. A five-minute period of think time is provided before beginning the protocol so each group member can identify the topic they wish to present. There are three distinct parts of the conversation. Part One: One team member is the speaker for five or six minutes while the other two or three listen attentively and record key ideas. The two or three listeners identify one person to paraphrase and ask clarifying questions. Part Two: Once the team member's speaking concludes, the two or three listeners spend two or three minutes verbally providing the key ideas the speaker identified. Part Three: The two or three listeners spend three or four minutes providing suggestions or feedback if the speaker requests it. This process is repeated until all group members have had the opportunity to be the speaker. The process takes thirty to forty minutes to complete.

Table 14. The CANAM Team Protocol
Part One: Communication Pattern of Paraphrasing and Posing Questions

Paraphrasing	A key skill in listening attentively. Communicates that the listener understood what was said. It takes practice and is a summary of key ideas rather than a verbatim summary.

Posing Questions	Used to gain clarity or stimulate further thinking. Questions are invitational, open-ended, and not advice in disguise. Example: Can you tell us more about…? What did you mean when you said…?

Part Two: Feedback for Adult Learning and Growth

Specific	Data or information needs to be tangible and clear and cannot be implied, vague, or general.
Manageable	Feedback needs to be simple. Cognitive load—the amount of information being processed—must be monitored.
Factual	Data and agreed-upon information are shared. Opinions and criticism are not communicated because they negatively impact a feedback relationship.
Alterable	Feedback focuses on alterable behaviors that can be changed and adjusted, and not personal characteristics.

Part Three: Structure for the Conversation

Step One	One team member speaks for five or six minutes on an identified topic. The other two or three team members record key ideas. One member is designated to paraphrase and pose questions.
Step Two	Once the team member's speaking concludes, the two or three listeners spend two or three minutes summarizing the key ideas the speaker identified.
Step Three	If the speaker requests feedback or suggestions, the two or three listeners spend three of four minutes providing solicited feedback for adult learning and growth.

Professional conversations that focus on growth and feedback require skills and structures different from normal conversations. It was the CAGIS Foundation team's observation with our mentoring work that under the correct circumstances and in a trusting, professional relationship when expertise is shared, the learning of a new set of skills can be accelerated dramatically. Many professionals yearn for words of support and encouragement. The CANAM Team Protocol is a tool that can be adjusted and used in most professional settings. The CAGIS team finds this protocol helpful when planning an involved task or a meeting with many moving parts. We used it several times to plan the event you are attending today.

Chapter Five:
Questions to Engage Your Thinking and for Discussion or Dialogue with Colleagues

Nora states that we all have the capacity to learn about ourselves, and when we do, it is usually hard-earned through the successes and failures of experience in our work and private lives.

1. What "hard-earned" learning have you experienced due to the successes and/or failures in your professional life?

Based on Nora's experiences providing professional development and training, she believes that the professionals who benefited the most when seeking support and feedback were those leaders who were humble enough to recognize that a willingness to accept constructive feedback accelerated their acquisition of professional expertise. Nora states, "Humility is not the absence of a strong sense of self; it is the ability to recognize our own strengths and weaknesses."

2. How do Nora's statements on humility and its role in accelerating the acquisition of expertise fit with your thoughts and perspective on humility?

3. Self-confidence is a characteristic traditionally attributed to successful leaders. What do you see as the relationship(s) or interplay between humility and self-confidence? How do these concepts relate to self-knowledge and self-awareness?

Nora notes that it takes practice and self-discipline to learn how to provide useful feedback that is constructive.

4. Which practices and protocols described by Nora would be most useful to you in learning how to provide useful feedback that is constructive?

Chapter Six

DAY FIVE—Adaptive Competence, from La Conner Harbor to Mosquito Creek Marina

Lincoln Angiak Presents

I am Lincoln Angiak, and I grew up in the village of Quinhagak, Alaska, on the Kanektok (Qanirtuuq in Yup'ik) River, a tributary of the Kuskokwim River. Quinhagak is located on the eastern shore of Kuskokwim Bay, about one mile from the Bering Sea coastline. My paternal grandparents, Bertha and Samuel, spoke English, Russian, and Yup'ik. Grandma Bertha was from Kongiganak, a small village on the western side of Kuskokwim Bay. It is about thirty air miles from Quinhagak, the home village of Grandpa Samuel. My grandparents were sent to and met at a Bureau of Indian Affairs high school in Oklahoma. Grandpa Samuel told me that some of the teachers attempted to have him unlearn many aspects of Yup'ik culture and focus on Western knowledge and beliefs.

My earliest memories are of being in *fish camp* on the Kuskokwim River for the summer catching, drying, and smoking salmon for the winter. I learned to operate a skiff in my early teens setting gillnets in channels of the Kuskokwim where salmon were swimming upriver. We would fish for the most sought-after species of salmon, kings, in June. Chum and silver salmon were fished in July and August. Salmon are an essential food for Yup'ik people and a subsistence and communal way of life. In the summer, I went to the village only when we needed to transport salmon or retrieve supplies and fuel. I preferred being on the river.

Grandpa Samuel attended St. Herman Russian Orthodox Seminary in Kodiak, Alaska, when I was a teenager. He participated in a program to become a church deacon during winter when our family was not commercial or subsistence fishing. I had the opportunity to visit my grandparents in Kodiak during spring break when I was a junior in high school. I received a tour of Coast Guard Base Kodiak during my visit. It is the Coast Guard's largest operational base and the only base to support cutters and aircraft. The Coast Guard motto Semper Paratus (Always Ready) made sense because the *coasties*, or Coast Guard members assigned to Coast Guard Base Kodiak, are responsible for aerial search and rescue of over 4 million square miles.

I had an affinity for fishing in the Kuskokwim River system for salmon and the Bering Sea for halibut. My Uncle Oscar served in the US Navy and encouraged me to make a living on the water. Oscar noticed that I wanted to learn more about how to become a skipper aboard the barges and tugs that navigated the Kuskokwim River. I enlisted in the US Coast Guard after graduating from high school. Once I completed training, I was assigned to the USCGC *Alex Haley*, which was stationed at Coast Guard Base Kodiak. Few people recognize that Yup'ik people have one of the highest rates of service per capita in the military of any demographic group in the United States.[29] I felt like I was participating in a tradition of service to our country by the Yup'ik people.

I served in the Coast Guard for four years and was honorably discharged from active military service as a boatswain's mate first class. A boatswain can perform almost any task aboard a vessel, which makes this job very marketable in civilian life. The experiences in the Coast Guard prepared me for continuing a path toward being a tugboat captain. I appreciated being a coastie, and like many who serve, I decided to not continue because I wanted to be home more frequently. I was especially fortunate to be employed by Sainte-Foy Marine, Ltd. and assigned to Alyeska Tug and Barge in North Vancouver. I applied to participate in Sainte-Foy Marine's first-generation mariners program and almost immediately formed a professional and personal relationship with Jean-Philippe. The program supplemented my income by paying for any training and US Coast Guard licenses I wanted to obtain.

I obtained US Coast Guard licenses for Master of Towing for Oceans, Near Coastal, and Western Rivers. I was the first mate aboard the *Nordic Quest,* which was captained by Marit-Abril. She was a superb mentor and a kindred spirit because of our common life experiences of fishing for salmon in Alaska. I discovered a person who was a thoughtful and careful listener, like the way of my family and Yup'ik people. It has been my experience that most people are not curious or aware of how those different from themselves view the world. Marit-Abril and I were interested in each other's stories, experiences, and beliefs.

I left the *Nordic Quest* to become the skipper of the *Kusko,* a self-propelled, double-hulled barge that delivered supplies and fuel to the small villages along the Kuskokwim River. I was finally home, working on the river that was a part of my spirit. Marit-Abril was now the captain of the oceangoing tugboat *Katmai,* which delivered fuel to the tank farm in Bethel. We had the opportunity to rendezvous in Quinhagak. The *Kusko* was delivering fuel and freight from Bethel to Quinhagak, and the *Katmai* was towing fuel from the tank farm in Dutch Harbor to the tank farm in Bethel. I had shared with Marit-Abril the internal conflict of not feeling like I could easily fit into my traditional Yup'ik culture, the Russian Orthodox Eastern culture, and the Western culture that was my work life. I believe that we can begin to understand each other when we open ourselves up and experience firsthand just a small part of the lives we hope to understand.

It was during this common experience that Marit-Abril could now understand my internal conflict, and I was able to clearly express the challenge of trying to adapt to multiple ways of being in the world simultaneously. My grandparents and parents discouraged my brother Lewis and me from talking about ourselves in ways that might appear arrogant. It was stressed not to focus on oneself in both Yup'ik culture and in the Russian Orthodox Church, where Grandpa Samuel was a deacon in his later years at St. Gabriel Church in Kongiganak. The belief in humbly walking made it difficult to write about myself even though the CAGIS Foundation team encouraged me to detail some of my family histories because the topic I will cover today is about being adaptive.

Jean-Philippe had suggested that I could play an integral role, if I were interested, in establishing an Alyeska Tug and Barge presence in the Canadian Arctic. It was an intriguing offer since one goal of this venture was to support vessels experimenting with green hydrogen as a power supply. Hydrogen that is not produced from fossil fuels would be an important development for Yup'ik people living in rural Alaska who are totally dependent on fossil fuels. We are dependent on fossil fuels with few viable alternatives in the foreseeable future.

The coastal Alaska villages of Newtok, Kivalina, and Shishmaref are three of the many considering migration or relocation due to climate change.[30] The immediate concern I have for my family and village outweighed the desire to participate as a tugboat captain for Alyeska Tug and Barge in the Canadian Arctic. My village, Quinhagak, is one of over two dozen villages discussing relocation due to climate change. Erosion and thawing permafrost threaten Quinhagak's multipurpose building, airstrip, water treatment plant, sewer lagoon, laundromat, and health clinic. The situation is dire because the impact of warming temperatures on the most vulnerable people geographically and economically results in few viable options without immediate intervention and significant financial assistance.

I declined Jean-Philippe's offer because I felt compelled to explore the resources that might help Quinhagak. I was working from Vancouver in the winter months after the *Kusko* summer delivery schedule was completed. I had ample time off and access to the resources of Sainte-Foy Marine and Alyeska Tug and Barge on the North Shore Waterfront. I had established good relationships with numerous tribes and First Nations while seeking candidates for the first-generation and underrepresented minorities for Sainte-Foy Marine's mariners' program.

It surprised me to learn that many tribal organizations had already responded to climate change for over a decade using scientific data and the insights of Traditional Ecological Knowledge (TEK). The Swinomish Indian Tribe was generous and welcoming in my quest to help Quinhagak. The Swinomish Indian Reservation is about 90 miles southeast of North Vancouver, near where we are today, with Similk Bay and Kiket Bay to the west, Marthas Bay to the south, and the Swinomish Channel to the east. Tribal organizations such as the Swinomish Indian Tribal Community realize they are vulnerable to the consequences of climate change and are leading the way in creating *climate action plans.*

We have spent the past four days learning about the CAGIS *Dispositions of Leadership.* One of the first major steps for each team after we conclude this five-day journey together will be to engage your constituents in the process of beginning the development of climate action plans. Before we leave port, we thought it would be beneficial to learn about the Swinomish Indian Tribal Community's climate change action plans. We are docked at La Conner, Washington, and you can see many of the Swinomish Village buildings from the back deck of the RV *Smart Ports.* Before setting sail for our destination, where we will discuss the fifth and final CAGIS Disposition of Leadership, we will be the invited guests of the Swinomish Indian Tribe for a presentation of the *Swinomish Climate Change Initiative Climate Adaptation Action Plan.*[31] The 90-page plan represents a model of collaborating with partners and the wisdom of creating a viable and healthy environment for future generations. I am confident that we will all learn a lot from the graciousness of the Swinomish Indian Tribe in spending some time with us this morning.

Keystone Disposition: Adaptive Competence

Now that we've heard the Swinomish Indian Tribe's remarkably interesting and thought-provoking presentation, I look forward to the conversations that will happen over lunch later today as we share our thoughts about the *Swinomish Climate Change Initiative Climate Adaptation Action Plan*. For now, however, we will proceed to the last of the CAGIS *Dispositions of Leadership, Adaptive Competence* as we set off to our final port.

I have been fortunate to be a part of the CAGIS Foundation team in so many ways that I cannot imagine a personal and professional life without them. Erika Knudsen, with her background in cognitive science, shared resources about how different cultures approach learning and adapting. I was able to share my Indigenous knowledge, or Traditional Ecological Knowledge (TEK), with Erika, and it influenced how she thinks about learning. Traditional Ecological Knowledge was not represented in the professional academic literature that Erika utilized during her university career. Collaboratively, we were able to craft a definition of Adaptive Competence in Textbox 2 that has broad application.[32] It is my hope you can work in similar ways to harness the skills and talents of all your team members.

Textbox 2. Broad Definition of Adaptive Competence

> *Adaptive Competence* is the ability to utilize knowledge and insights acquired from past situations and determine how to apply those insights flexibly and creatively in novel or unfamiliar settings.[33]

This fifth and final disposition, Adaptive Competence, is the keystone disposition that will assist your coastal zone teams who are responsible for leading the development of a climate action plan in two important ways. First, it is especially important that we understand *how* to think about the complex problems that we will encounter. Second, establishing the approaches for addressing complex problems will require *modeling flexibility*. The two bulleted lists in Table 15 provide the capabilities and key practices of Adaptive Competence.

Table 15. Disposition: Adaptive Competence

CAPABILITY: Understand and analyze complex problems
PRACTICES:
• Utilize current knowledge and apply it in a novel setting
• Develop the capacity to diagnose aspects of presenting problems
• Apply from the *bridge* view and on the *deck* view
• Understand and address technical problems and adaptive challenges
• Unbundle aspects of a problem while keeping the whole in mind
• Prioritize areas of focus and consider which areas might need attention first
CAPABILITY: Engage in flexible thinking to address complex problems

PRACTICES:
• Be willing to modify approaches based upon evidence
• Develop alternative strategies when adaptive challenges are encountered
• Model patience while designing potential solutions
• Communicate that problems are not intractable
• Seek and listen to diverse views

There are two key concepts that are helpful when confronted with a situation, challenge, or problem, and we want to diagnose accurately. The first concept is understanding the analogy of having *the bridge* view and *the deck* view when we encounter problems or decisions.[34] We need to find a space to assess a situation or diagnose a problem, like a view on the bridge of a ship. The bridge has instruments and a 180-degree view for observing and diagnosing a situation. The bridge provides the view to accurately assess and understand a situation and gather needed information before deciding how to respond. The view *from the bridge* lessens the possibility we will react reflexively. In contrast, the *view on the deck* is for actively influencing a situation. The idea of acting and being decisive must be balanced by considering the possibility of unintended consequences that might happen with direct involvement.

The second key concept is understanding the distinction between *technical problems* and *adaptive challenges*.[35] A common vocabulary for describing the work that is in front of us is enormously useful when developing and implementing a climate action plan. Technical problems can be addressed by utilizing the knowledge and expertise already in place. Adaptive challenges require learning new ideas and even revising our behavior.[36]

As an example of technical problems, I will share with you my experiences when I assumed command of the *Kusko*. The *Kusko* was a brand-new tugboat equipped with state-of-the-art navigational instruments and a first-generation engine system. The *Nordic Quest,* the boat I left for my new tug, was much larger and built in the 1980s with upgrades consistent with its design. I knew how to operate a tugboat, and any problems encountered while transitioning to the *Kusko* were technical in nature. The crew and I were able to update our knowledge base quickly because we already had an extensive understanding of tugboat instruments and power supplies. Fortunately, in this instance, we were able to resolve any of these *technical problems* we encountered quickly. We launched the *Kusko* from drydock and completed our first trip without incident.

Adaptive challenges are not resolved quickly like these technical problems aboard the *Kusko*. Adaptive challenges require prioritizing possible actions and a willingness to adjust based on information and feedback. An example from my experiences of adaptive challenges makes me think of the village of Quinhagak, which is confronted with the possibility of rebuilding or relocating due to rising water levels and thawing tundra. Many of the challenges facing my family in Quinhagak will be adaptive challenges. These challenges will require new patterns of individual and group behavior that will hopefully reduce erosion and minimize the impact of thawing tundra.

Capability: Engage in Flexible Thinking to Address Complex Problems

There are numerous problem-solving processes and strategies that teams can use when addressing an adaptive challenge or complex problem. The premise behind most problem-solving strategies is to identify and understand the challenge, explore options, devise an action plan, and adjust based on data and feedback. It is shortsighted to think that presenting hard data as a single area of focus will be sufficient when addressing an adaptive challenge. Problem-solving processes that present a linear and logical model work well when solving technical problems but are not sufficient to address adaptive challenges. The problem-solving processes currently working for your team in addressing technical problems might need to be adjusted when an adaptive challenge is encountered.

Data about rising sea levels and warming temperatures are indisputable facts. Collecting and sharing data establishes a rationale and a starting point to reevaluate where we live and how we interact with our environment. The overwhelming evidence of rising sea levels makes rational sense, and it might seem like it should be enough to motivate people to act. However, adaptive challenges can be hard to address because *extensive changes* in human behavior over an *extended period* can be overwhelming and arduous.[37] How a group might respond to altering their pattern of existence is grounded in emotion and identity. This is especially true when people are not simply *living on* the land; they are *connected to* the entire environment in ways that are ineffable.

A straightforward rational approach to problem-solving might need to be adjusted when emotion and identity are at the forefront. The CANAM Norms of listening, equal status, and the predictable values of integrity, transparency, and honesty are essential when engaging a group confronted with adaptive challenges. The teams here today need to make evidence-based decisions while recognizing the need to *be in positive and reciprocal relationships* with members of their respective communities. Teams need to anticipate the implications of emotion and identity when addressing adaptive challenges.

Technical Problems, Adaptive Challenges, and Manageable Dilemmas

There are specific topics that need to be communicated when addressing adaptive challenges. Many, or perhaps most, decisions that require adaptability are not simple or easy to implement. They require setting priorities and a willingness to adjust and even experiment with potential solutions. In other words, we need to foster an environment for applying the attributes of being adaptively competent. It is essential to communicate those problems as not intractable. Some potential solutions might be unpalatable, but this is different than thinking a problem is unsolvable.

We do face dilemmas that are not readily solvable. For example, balancing the time at sea to earn an income with the obligations of being ashore with family is something that must be managed and is not readily solvable. (Unless, of course, you quit the seagoing job.) It is commonly referred to as work/life balance. Another example is that we will all encounter the reality of centralized authority and control that needs to be balanced with the realization that any local decision-making requires a meaningful level of flexibility. This type of interjurisdictional coordination will be in play for all grant participants and is an example of a manageable dilemma—it is a problem or challenge that cannot be solved per se but rather needs to be acknowledged and addressed as an ongoing dilemma managed over time.[38]

One of the important things for us to do as a team is to tease out and identify technical problems, adaptive challenges, and manageable dilemmas so that we understand what we are trying to address. It is possible that as we examine the situations, there will be elements of all three simultaneously.

Modify Approaches and Develop Alternative Strategies

It is essential to ask team members to withhold judgment when exploring alternative strategies or when modifying an approach that is already established. We live in a world where the default position in many situations is an immediate rush to judgment. A hallmark of groups that address adaptive challenges effectively is the ability to honor knowledge previously acquired while demonstrating a willingness to explore new information. Two unhelpful positions for a team member to assert are: 1) disregarding previous actions before understanding them, and 2) an unwillingness to consider changing past practices. A team seeking to eliminate or modify current approaches to a situation or develop alternative strategies is well served by utilizing the four questions in Table 16.

Members of the CAGIS Foundation team developed Table 16, and it was inspired by Jean-Philippe when he was working with a group on developing *Sleek Surface Maritime* hull coating. Jean-Philippe discovered using tentative words like *might* to promote thinking was most helpful when using the four questions as "deck rails" to tighten the process. (Deck rails on a ship provide a boundary while still allowing freedom of movement.) When brainstorming is an open-ended, freewheeling activity, progress toward identifying potential solutions can be elusive. Deck rails are needed to provide some boundaries while not restricting creativity and the possibilities of innovative ideas.

Table 16. Questions for Modifying Approaches and Forming Alternative Strategies

Four Questions Using Tentative Language	Topic and Rationale/ Reasoning
Why might we maintain a strategy or practice?	
Why might we adjust a current strategy or practice?	
Why might we eliminate a strategy or practice?	
Why might we adopt a new strategy or practice?	

We invite you to use Table 16 during future deliberations. A consideration is to have a silent writing time responding to the topic and rationale reasoning column of the table before verbal responses begin. It has been the experience of CAGIS Foundation team members that the sequence of think, write, respond promotes a higher quality conversation. Also, the conversation should be constructed as a dialogue and not a discussion. As a reminder, earlier in this journey, we talked about the differences between discussion and dialogue. *Discussion* is used when options are identified, choices are determined, and a decision is made. In contrast, *dialogue* is a type of conversation where ideas are explored, decision-making is suspended, and the collective understanding is the hoped-for outcome.[39] Therefore, dialogue is critical to effectively addressing adaptive challenges.

Model Patience and Listen to Diverse Views

I find it much easier to talk about patience than to model it when working with groups. The first two statements noted on the CANAM Norms Defined Table 3 model patience when we pause to attend to what is said and when we paraphrase to communicate that we understand what was said by the speaker. It is always a good practice to provide all team members an opportunity to make a verbal contribution. "I pass" is an acceptable contribution if someone prefers not to comment. We invite diverse views when we model patience, listen, and encourage participation by all team members. Our time for learning and exploring the CAGIS *Dispositions of Leadership* is nearly complete, and I would like to point out that we are ending almost at the point where we started: by encouraging the uniquely human characteristic of listening to understand others.

Adaptive Competence in Leadership

The significant challenge for coastal communities impacted by rising sea levels and more intense weather events is developing responses that are as proactive as possible. The CAGIS Foundation team observes that it is not wise to narrowly describe adaptation as a physical change or adjustment that is made in response to the environment. A broader definition of human adaptation is needed as the rate of change increases due to the explosion of information and the rapid change to the natural world because of our warming planet. More consideration will need to be given to how humans might adapt physically, psychologically, and emotionally to a rapidly changing and complex world.

The five CAGIS *Dispositions of Leadership* were designed as a framework to use when complex problems and adaptive challenges confront us. Adaptive competence is the keystone disposition because to apply the capabilities and practices identified in the other four dispositions, adaptive competence must be in place. A keystone is the final piece of stone placed at the top of an arch, which locks all the stones into position. Without the keystone, the entire structure will not stand. Textbox 3 provides a narrower definition of Adaptive Competence than was presented in Textbox 2. The definition in Textbox 3 specifically considers the CAGIS Foundation team's leadership work and the five *Dispositions of Leadership*.

Textbox 3. CAGIS Leadership Definition of Adaptive Competence

> *Adaptive Competence* is the ability to assess and diagnose a specific situation, determine which *Dispositions of Leadership* practices will be helpful, and *implement them collaboratively as a team.*

The CAGIS Foundation team invites you to consider reviewing the CAGIS *Dispositions of Leadership* with the intention of selecting those practices that will assist your team in becoming more effective and efficient. The CAGIS Foundation team has a tradition of eating Chinese food while in Vancouver, and it is a useful analogy for focusing on a few things that will help your team. Dim sum is a style of eating where carts are wheeled through the restaurant, and you select from as many as forty or fifty items. All the dishes look delicious, and it is impossible to eat all of them. The friends or family at each table discuss the items they would like to eat. The selections made by people at each table can be vastly different because the groups make unique decisions.

We invite you to use the dim sum analogy as you review all the materials from this past week. The handouts and tables are organized by the dispositions and in the sequence presented:

- Communicating to Understand and to Influence
- Interdependent Thinking and Acting
- Gathering Information for Improvement and Innovation
- Seeking Support and Feedback
- Adaptive Competence

The four questions noted in Table 16 might provide an approach for examining and adjusting the strategies and processes your team currently uses in your work.

Earlier today, you had the unique opportunity to listen to the Swinomish tribal members discuss elements of their action plan that have been in place for over a decade. The final task of today is for each team to review the *Swinomish Climate Change Initiative Climate Adaptation Action Plan*. One of the lenses we would like you to consider using as you review the plan is to identify the topics in the plan that appear to be technical problems, adaptive challenges, or manageable dilemmas. Please remember a topic or item can have a combination of all three. The Table 17 Worksheet for Examining an Initiative is available for use as your team reviews the climate change and adaptation document.

Table 17. Worksheet for Examining an Initiative

Topic	Attributes	Climate Change Initiative Topic and Page
Technical Problem	Resolved quickly and can be addressed with a direct problem-solving approach	
Adaptive Challenge	Physical, emotional, and psychological adaptions are in play. Takes time to incorporate new information with past practices. Experimentation and adjustments might be needed	
Manageable Dilemma	Not solvable and can only be managed. Typical problem-solving approaches are unhelpful.	

Unfortunately, as we approach Mosquito Creek Marina in North Vancouver, our time together aboard the RV *Smart Ports* is coming to an end. But this does not at all imply that our time together has ended; far from it. The CANAM Smart Ports and Harbors Program will require that we all continue to communicate frequently and share information transparently. At times this will happen in real time, during face-to-face regional meetings or convenings with all grantee teams. Other times we may meet virtually or asynchronously when meetings are not scheduled. Remember, our collective mission is to reduce the impact of severe weather events and rising sea levels on our immediate communities by developing and implementing sustainable and adaptable practices. This can only be accomplished if we continue to collaborate and network, continue to share our knowledge and insights with one another, and continue to improve our plans and the outcomes for our communities.

I know that I speak for the entire CAGIS Foundation team when I state that we are extremely excited about the work that lies ahead for all of us with the CANAM Smart Ports and Harbors Program. And I would be remiss if I did not also say that we are honored, privileged, and grateful for the opportunity to work with such an amazing group of seafarers and colleagues.

Chapter Six:
Questions to Engage Your Thinking and for Discussion or Dialogue with Colleagues

---

Lincoln presents the idea of having the *bridge* view. He asserts that you need the view from the bridge of a ship to accurately assess and understand a situation and gather needed information before deciding how to respond.

1. Reflecting on recent work or personal situation, in what ways did you assess the situation from the bridge, and in what ways did you assess the situation from on the deck? What was the value of each respective view?

2. How might incorporating views from the bridge help you in your work or personal life?

3. Can you identify a time in your personal or work life when you were dealing with an adaptive challenge? Which of these characteristics accurately describe the adaptive challenge?

4. How might you be better able to address adaptive challenges in your work if you recognized emotional and psychological considerations are present?

Lincoln asserts that one of the important things to do as a team is to tease out and identify technical problems, adaptive challenges, and manageable dilemmas so that you understand what you are trying to address. Technical problems can usually be addressed via an action plan. Adaptive challenges require balancing new information while applying problem-solving strategies to manage a dilemma.

5. How might your work be different if you took the time to tease out and identify technical problems, adaptive challenges, and manageable dilemmas before responding to problems or issues in your work or personal life?

6. Reflecting on your current or past work experiences, are there times that you misidentified a manageable dilemma and tried to apply problem-solving strategies? What was the outcome? How might the experience and outcome have been different if you had better understood what you were trying to address?

Adaptive Competence is the keystone disposition because *Adaptive Competence* must be in place to apply the capabilities and practices identified in the other four dispositions. A keystone is the final piece of stone placed at the top of a structure, and it locks all the stones into position. Without the keystone, the entire structure will not stand.

7. How do you view Adaptive Competence as being the key disposition for "locking all the stones [dispositions] into position"? What is the relationship between adaptive competence and the other four dispositions?

8. To what extent do you agree or disagree with the assertion that without Adaptive Competence, "the entire structure will not stand"?

9. Please refer to Appendix C for an opportunity to actively participate as a team member of the BC Coastal Communities Climate Change Alliance. The alliance represents the Port of Vancouver, British Columbia, and Steveston Harbour on the Fraser River and Nanaimo Harbour, on Vancouver Island, British Columbia. The team is deliberating over how to utilize the capabilities and practices from the disposition Adaptive Competence.

Chapter Seven

The CAGIS Foundation Team Debrief

Departures and Dim Sum

There was an air of excitement and brightness despite the dreary, rainy weather as everyone disembarked the *RV Smart Ports* at Mosquito Creek Marina in North Vancouver. The CANAM Smart Ports and Harbors Program grant participants, many (or most) of whom had only met for the first time five days earlier, shared a powerful bond that defied the length of their relationships. It was the type of powerful bond often experienced after such intensive training, a bond, and camaraderie intensified by both the structure and content of the training. The CAGIS Foundation team had "walked the talk," enacting and modeling the very capabilities and practices that they presented to the participants, such as the use of meeting norms foundational for interacting and communicating in a constructive manner and using the practices from Developing Personal Presence to cultivate trust and collaboration in working relationships. These practices and protocols made the five-day training productive, established strong relationships between the participants and laid the foundation for ongoing networks of colleagues bonded by common understandings and goals.

Slowly, everyone dispersed, and the lingering farewells between participants between the CAGIS Foundation team and the participants drew to a close. Marit-Abril, Erika, Nora, Lincoln, and Jean-Philippe remained behind at the marina and decided to share a meal before getting some much-needed sleep at a local bed and breakfast. Lincoln, still thinking about his presentation that day when he made the dim sum analogy, had a strong craving for Chinese food. The roots of Vancouver's Asian cuisine were more than a century deep, and Vancouver had developed notoriety as an Asian food paradise. Marit-Abril, Jean-Philippe, Nora, and Erika wholeheartedly endorsed heading to a local Chinese restaurant run by fourth-generation Cantonese immigrants who adapted traditional Chinese recipes to Western tastes and the available ingredients. Traditionally dim sum was enjoyed in restaurants for breakfast and lunch, but fortunately for the five team members, it had become more commonplace over time for restaurants to serve dim sum at dinner too. Dim sum literally translates to "touching heart," which seemed very appropriate given the strong friendships between these five CAGIS Foundation team members.

As the steam-heated carts came by their table, Marit-Abril, Erika, Nora, Lincoln, and Jean-Philippe enjoyed a casual and light conversation about the five-day training aboard the RV *Smart Ports*. Even before arriving at the restaurant, the team had agreed they would not engage in dialogue *or* discussion that evening about the impact and outcomes of the training. The team did believe in "walking the talk," but there would be time for those other things when they met the next morning to formally debrief. The five team members were exhausted and wanted to simply enjoy the broad range of flavors, textures, cooking styles, and ingredients while conversing with dear friends. Marit-Abril, Erika, Nora, Lincoln, and Jean-Philippe lingered over their food that evening as they selected from the weekly specials, house signature dishes, and seasonal offerings. The room filled with laughter and joy as they shared food, fun, and conversation.

The Formal Debrief

Although all team members were well versed in these topics both conceptually and in practice, Jean-Philippe wanted to ensure that the team had visible reminders of the keys for effective team collaboration. The CAGIS Foundation team only had one day together in person for the formal debrief, and no one wanted to waste time. The team would enact what they had presented to the CANAM Smart Ports and Harbors Program grant participants: the meeting would be well facilitated, structured for balanced participation, and have clearly stated goals, outcomes, and success criteria.

As they began their day, Marit-Abril reflected that, in essence, the purpose of the debrief meeting was one of the five CAGIS *Dispositions of Leadership*, Gathering Information for Improvement and Innovation. They were gathering at the Wheelhouse to review information about the impact and effectiveness of the five-day leadership training in meeting its intended goals and purposes. Marit-Abril reminded everyone that the original goal of the leadership training was for all participating organizations in the grant to form a common purpose and focus on agreed-upon tangible goals. The intended short-term outcomes of the leadership training included: increasing grantees' understanding of and commitment to the mission of the CANAM Smart Ports and Harbors Program; increasing grantees' knowledge, understanding, and use of the CAGIS *Dispositions of Leadership*; providing grantees with a common mindset and a common language needed for supporting one another and collaborating on common goals and objectives; and creating an interdependent network of grantees (and group identity) that would support one another and allow them to share their collective expertise.

Marit-Abril, Nora, Erika, Lincoln, and Jean-Philippe spent the day engaging in dialogue about their perceptions of the impact and effectiveness of the five-day leadership training regarding these intended short-term outcomes. Although these data were anecdotal, the five team members found it invaluable to share their perceptions. The specifics of the information gathered for improvement and feedback on that specific debriefing day at the Wheelhouse are superfluous in terms of describing the *Leadership Voyage* of Marit-Abril and her colleagues and would add another few hundred pages to this narrative. Suffice it to say that successes were noted, and equally, the team members identified areas for improvement. What was significant about the debriefing meeting that day was that they were "walking the talk" within an environment of trust, honesty, integrity, transparency, and the broader framework of common understandings and goals.

The formal debrief that day was only one small component of the CAGIS Foundation team's focus on Gathering Information for Improvement and Innovation on the impact and effectiveness of the five-day leadership training. Data were also gathered via participant surveys that went beyond asking about the food and room temperature to gather data on participants' perceived knowledge, understanding, and skills related to the five-day training. And these data were also supplemented by qualitative interviews with some of the participants from each grant team.

The debrief was just one component of the team's Gathering Information for Improvement and Innovation review of the five-day leadership training. Looking at the debrief meeting was akin to viewing Gathering Information for Improvement and Innovation *from the deck*. Whereas the *view from the bridge* would allow you to see the breadth and depth of how Marit-Abril, Lincoln, Erika, Nora, and Jean-Philippe integrated the continuous and comprehensive Gathering Information for Improvement and Innovation into the CANAM Smart Ports and Harbors Program. The debrief was only one small but important piece of the larger plan.

Indeed, the *view from the bridge* takes us away from our *view from the deck* of this one-day debrief in the Wheelhouse. The CAGIS Foundation team was fully committed to evidence-based decision-making, and they had fully integrated throughout the life of the grant gathering and reporting *quantitative* and *qualitative* data, developing an environment of open-minded inquiry for continuous improvement, and using data to inform decisions and actions. Improvement and innovation were critical to the success of the CANAM Smart Ports and Harbors Program, so much so that the CAGIS Foundation team also employed an external evaluator to partner in Gathering Information for Improvement and Innovation.

Based on her experience with evaluation, one of Erika's first suggestions upon being invited to join the CAGIS Foundation team was that the foundation should use an external evaluator to gather the types of valid and reliable quantitative and qualitative data needed to inform policy and decision-making. Erika emphasized the importance of an external evaluation entity not only because of the added value of their expertise in evaluation research but also because of the different lens and objectivity that external evaluators bring to a project. The other four team members quickly agreed to devote the resources needed to contract with an external evaluator.

On Erika's recommendation, the CAGIS Foundation contracted with the Center for Evaluation, Policy, and Research (CEPR) at Indiana University in Bloomington. Erika noted that despite their Midwest home base, which was landlocked, CEPR had extensive experience nationally and internationally. In fact, Erika described a comprehensive statewide evaluation that a colleague of hers at CEPR had conducted throughout Alaska, including site visits near Lincoln's home village in the Kuskokwim River delta. These site visits included traveling from Bethel, a commercial center and medium draft port on the Kuskokwim River, to remote bush (rural) villages via a seasonal ice road that connects more than 11,000 people in more than 15 bush communities.

Lincoln shared that it was beneficial to have grant evaluators who understood that the Alaska State Department of Transportation does not consider river ice roads part of the state's transportation infrastructure because they are not permanent. However, these plowed ice roads range from 200 to 399 miles long, depending on the conditions and resources in any given year, allowing for snow machines and trucks in a region that otherwise relies on unpredictable airplane travel in winter. Unfortunately, these ice roads that are critical for medical aid, food supplies, and fuel for remote Indigenous communities are also being impacted by climate change. Remote Indigenous communities are disproportionately threatened as winters grow warmer, causing seasonal ice roads to freeze later in the fall (or early winter), thaw earlier in the spring, and become less stable throughout the winter. Lincoln suggested that grant evaluators who took the time to understand the people impacted by climate change would be valued team members.

Marit's Abril's Reflections

In the weeks since she and her CAGIS Foundation colleagues parted, Marit-Abril frequently reflected on her experiences aboard the RV *Smart Ports*, and she shared with them her personal and professional perspectives about the voyage. She spent a good amount of time during the debriefing and afterward discussing the impact and effectiveness of the five-day leadership training with Lincoln, Erika, Nora, and Jean-Philippe and the next steps for the CANAM Smart Ports and Harbors Program. Things were moving ahead smoothly. Gaps that had not been addressed via the five-day leadership training were identified, new plans were developed, new goals were set, virtual meetings with grantees were conducted, CEPR continued gathering evaluation data, and the five core CAGIS Foundation team members continued to engage in ongoing dialogue and discussions several times a week as they moved forward with the CANAM Smart Ports and Harbors Program.

However, amid all this work with the CAGIS Foundation, Marit-Abril also spent time quietly reflecting on her personal and professional growth. She had recently commented to Lincoln on one of their video calls that "everything these days seems to come back to the *Dispositions of Leadership*—it's like there is no escaping them. They are everywhere." This seemed to hold true when Marit-Abril reflected on her experiences aboard the *RV Smart Ports*. In essence, in the language of the omnipresent *Dispositions of Leadership*, Marit-Abril was enveloped in the capability of developing self-knowledge and self-awareness (Disposition: Seeking Support and Feedback that Fosters Growth). Sometimes this disposition is addressed because of thoughtful, intentional, planned practices and protocols during a formal training or workshop. Other times, like in Marit-Abril's case, they just happened.

Marit-Abril thought back to Jean-Philippe's presentation while she was at Cal Maritime. The presentation was titled "Who I am, Who Will You Become, and What Might We Address for the Future of the Maritime Industry?" Although she heard the presentation many years before the CAGIS Foundation was even formed, she kept coming back to the questions posed by Jean-Philippe so long ago. She particularly remembered him saying, "I will ask you *who* you want to become and not *what* you aspire to do." She was struck at the time by how different this perspective was in looking at one's future. She realized that she could not even begin to count the number of times that she had been asked during her formative years by teachers, relatives, and friends, "What do you want to be when you grow up?"

Even into adulthood, Marit-Abril recalled being continually asked by family, colleagues, and mentors, "What do you want to do next?" As supportive as Marit-Abril's parents were of her maritime aspirations, even Tobias and Camilla frequently asked questions about *what* she aspired to do with her life. These questions and probes from family and others were well-intended, at least by caring friends and definitely by her parents. Yes, there were those like some old-timers at Cal Maritime who probed about aspirations in a manner that was less than supportive of women in the maritime industry, but generally, Marit-Abril had felt like her aspirations were supported by others in her life.

But reframing the question to *who* you want to become, rather than *what* you aspire to do, was a novel perspective for Marit-Abril to consider when she first heard Jean-Philippe speak those words many years ago. It was a life-changing moment for Marit-Abril, although she did not appreciate just how much so until many years later. In looking back, Marit-Abril realized that it was during that time that she first began to think about her future in terms of *who* she *chose* to be and how that would influence what would happen to her. Jean-Philippe's words helped her to realize that she played an active role in how her life would proceed and that she had a choice of *who* she would become in the years ahead. She remembered Jean-Philippe stating, "Character is first and foremost about *who we choose to be* and not *defining ourselves by a job title*."

Marit-Abril realized on that day when Jean-Philippe gave his presentation, albeit not consciously at the time, that *who* she wanted to become was an ethical, trustworthy, and empathetic seafarer with the integrity and moral purpose to assist those who are economically and environmentally marginalized due to climate change. And she wanted to be both humble and passionate in doing so. She now reflected back on her personal and professional experiences with this perspective on *who* she wanted to become: her earliest days in commercial fishing as a deckhand on the *Abril Mia,* assuming the role of captain of the *Abril Mia*, joining her cousin Erik to captain the *Nordic Dreki*, her expedition with NOAA researchers studying whales, her time as a tugboat skipper delivering freight and fuel to coastal and island communities north of Vancouver, BC, and throughout Southeast Alaska, as well as her current work with the CAGIS Foundation. She realized more than ever that no job titles or responsibilities, even her key role leading the CAGIS Foundation, defined *who* she was or *chose* to be.

In talking to Jean-Philippe about her revelations, Marit-Abril stated, "None of the roles themselves mattered; whether I was a deckhand or a captain or a leader of a major charitable foundation was largely irrelevant. What mattered was that throughout and across the various roles I assumed, *who* I was and *who* I was choosing to be remained the same—I was choosing to be an ethical, trustworthy, and empathetic seafarer with the integrity and moral purpose of assisting those economically and environmentally marginalized due to climate change. I was choosing to be both humble and passionate in doing so."

She also remembered Jean-Philippe asserting that we needed "to choose wisely the people who will support and mentor us" rather than "leaving the work of developing important character traits to chance, fate, or letting the busyness of our lives crowd out learning." That day she first heard Jean-Philippe say those words, she had made a conscious choice to intentionally seek out those people who could help her develop the character traits that would sustain her throughout her personal and professional lives. And that process began with the very person who spoke those words. Marit-Abril intentionally sought out Jean-Philippe as her mentor, colleague, and friend. Marit-Abril knew that intentionally and consciously seeking out that relationship with Jean-Philippe was one of her most important decisions in choosing *who* she would become.

Obviously, Nora, Lincoln, and Erika were the others she had intentionally sought out to help sustain her through her personal and professional lives. She was grateful for the choices she had made that led her to work with Jean-Philippe, Nora, Lincoln, and Erika. There were times in the past that she felt "lucky" to have developed such rich and rewarding relationships with such accomplished colleagues. But more recently, she had realized that it was not fate that brought them together but a series of choices that she was continuously making about *who* she wanted to be that formed and sustained those relationships with Jean-Philippe, Nora, Lincoln, and Erika.

It was during this time that Marit-Abril also realized that she thought about things a little bit differently than Jean-Philippe when he gave his presentation at Cal Maritime. She realized that from her perspective, the integral question was not "*who* will you become?" but rather "*who* will you be?" She believed the latter belied the ongoing and continuous nature of these questions and reflections and shifted the accountability for decisions. Marit-Abril thought that the question "who will you become?" made it too easy to not be accountable for your current actions and choices because the focus was always on the future. In contrast, Marit-Abril thought focusing on the question "who will you be?" focuses on intentional and conscious choices you make every day about your behaviors and actions.

As for Jean-Philippe's final question in his presentation, "What might we address for the future of the maritime industry?" Marit-Abril viewed this as the lifelong work of the CAGIS Foundation. She noted that, unfortunately, she was unsure that much progress had been made regarding climate change and the maritime industry in the years since Jean-Philippe gave that presentation at Cal Maritime. In many ways, it felt like the old cliché of "two steps forward, one step back." But she knew growth was not always linear and that the strong foundation they had laid for the CANAM Smart Ports and Harbors Program with the five-day leadership training was at least one (or possibly two) of those "steps forward."

More significantly, Marit-Abril passionately believed that the CANAM Smart Ports and Harbors Program would reach its goal of reducing the impact of severe weather events and rising sea levels on coastal communities by developing and implementing sustainable and adaptable practices. And she knew that the CAGIS *Dispositions of Leadership* would provide the needed framework for the success of the CANAM Smart Ports and Harbors Program, as well as the CAGIS Foundation more generally.

Marit-Abril did not know for sure exactly what roles and responsibilities she would have in the future with the CAGIS Foundation or what other job titles she might hold throughout her remaining years. It was an epiphany for Marit-Abril when she connected *being intentional in seeking support from trusted colleagues* with *recognizing personal growth and professional excellence are interconnected*. She now realized that Erika, the brilliant cognitive scientist, had helped the team knit together capabilities and practices that are inextricably intertwined. But she could answer one question with certainty, the question "*who* will I be?" Regardless of her job title or her career trajectory, she could state with certainty, "I will continue each day to choose to be an ethical, trustworthy, and empathetic seafarer; I will choose to have the integrity and moral purpose needed to assist those who are economically and environmentally marginalized due to climate change; and I will choose to be both humble and passionate in doing so."

Chapter Seven:
Questions to Engage Your Thinking and for Discussion or Dialogue with Colleagues

The formal debrief at the Wheelhouse essentially focused on Gathering Information for Improvement and Innovation on the impact and effectiveness of the five-day leadership training.

1. What are your thoughts and/or reactions to having just one of the *Dispositions of Leadership* serve as the focus of the debrief?

2. How might the technique of limiting the number of topics—the analogy of limiting the items selected from the dim sum carts—serve your team?

3. In what ways do you use debriefs in your professional life for Gathering Information for Improvement and Innovation?

Marit-Abril believed that the integral question was not "who will you become?" but rather "who will you be?" She thought that the question "who will you become?" made it too easy to not be accountable for your current actions and choices because it focuses on the future. In contrast, Marit-Abril thought focusing on the question "who will you be?" focuses on intentional and conscious choices you make every day about your behaviors and actions.

4. What are your thoughts about these two questions? Which one resonates more with you, and why?

5. How would you answer "who will you become?" or "who will you be?"

6. In what ways and to what extent do you define yourself by your job title(s) and/or what you aspire to be? How might your professional and personal life be different if you defined yourself by "who you will become" or "who you will be"?

Jean-Philippe's final question in his Cal Maritime presentation was: "What might we address for the future of the maritime industry?" Marit-Abril viewed this as the lifelong work of the CAGIS Foundation. She noted that, unfortunately, she was unsure that much progress had been made regarding climate change in the years since Jean-Philippe gave that presentation at Cal Maritime.

7. How do you view the progress made over the past twenty-five years with regards to climate change?

8. In what ways and to what extent do you see remote Indigenous communities as being disproportionately threatened by climate change? How can this be better addressed?

9. What do you see as the major obstacles or barriers to addressing critical climate change issues during the next ten years?

Appendix A
Communicating to Understand and to Influence

The Gulf Coast Sea Level Rise Consortium

The Port of Pascagoula, Mississippi, and the Harbors of Pascagoula and Biloxi, Mississippi

---

Your team members of the Gulf Coast Sea Level Rise Consortium requested that you present specific practices to implement from the disposition Communicating to Understand and to Influence. The group members asked you because of your past experiences facilitating groups. Your team is hoping to utilize helpful practices that result in efficient and effective meetings. An insight you learned from past experiences about effective meetings is that *group effectiveness* is directly related to the *interpersonal expertise of individual members*. An expectation of your team during this voyage is to learn new ideas and implement new practices.

During a lunch conversation, Marit-Abril Hansen, today's presenter, offered you a few ideas from her experiences while working on the CAGIS team. She suggested that introducing one or two practices at a time from the two capabilities increases the odds that group members can try new ideas without being overwhelmed. Marit-Abril also shared that the CAGIS team took a few minutes at the end of each meeting to reflect on how well they were integrating specific practices into their repertoire of skills. Marit-Abril shared "groups that reflect together are more likely to learn together." As the designated team facilitator, you decide to place Marit-Abril's quote in the "ideas" document. The document is a watermarked draft and states, "In keeping with the spirit of discovering new ways of being and new ways of doing: ideas for your consideration."

Your team's challenge is to identify *what* practices to implement from the list in this appendix and *how* to strategically go about utilizing them.

CAPABILITY: Develop Personal Presence (you)

Practices:

- Know and create conditions for being personally present (place aside distractions, monitor breathing)
- Be aware and alert to situations and contexts that require attentive listening
- Listen with undivided attention and empathy (monitor body language)
- Pause (demonstrate listening)
- Paraphrase (demonstrate understanding)
- Reframe negative language and model positivity
- Respond non-defensively and avoid sarcasm

CAPABILITY: Cultivate Productive Working Relationships (you and others)

Practices:

- Establish norms for interacting and communicating
- Develop working agreements and agendas
- Use discussion protocols and strategies for balanced participation
- Utilize strategies for encouraging dialogue and discussion
- Recognize and include diverse backgrounds and cultural perspectives

- Manage conflict proactively for healthy outcomes
- Seek constructive feedback to improve group performance

Appendix B
Interdependent Thinking and Acting

Nova Scotia Coastal Climate Collaborative

Port of Halifax and the Harbours of Halifax and Lunenburg, Nova Scotia, Canada

---

Jean-Philippe, today's presenter, shared some thoughts during lunch with your entire team about support for the overarching objectives and a shared understanding of group goals. These two topics were identified by your team, the Nova Scotia Coastal Climate Collaborative, for a deeper understanding. You offered to take notes during the conversation and facilitate a discussion later this evening during team time. The team members do not have a history of working together or previous experiences interacting with one another. However, their respective organizations have competed for grant funding and have had different philosophies and approaches to addressing sea-level increase.

When they applied for the CANAM Smart Ports and Harbors Program, all team members understood that collaboration and cooperation would be needed between the federal government, Mi'kmaq First Nations, provincial agencies, and local governmental organizations. The team had committed to learning new ideas and trying new practices during the voyage of leadership discovery aboard the RV *Smart Ports*. Jean-Philippe reinforced the notion that each group should focus only on the specific practices that would help propel them forward.

Jean-Philippe shared some of his hard-earned insights about interdependence when he led the *Sleek Surface Maritime* development team. Trust is the glue that holds a team together, especially when challenges are encountered. He asserted that all team members should have equal status and no individual is more or less important than their colleagues. Jean-Philippe shared that when he facilitates, he is the last person to speak during a discussion or a dialogue. He believes that deferring to colleagues is a powerful gesture that demonstrates each person's importance to the team. Jean-Phillippe learned that two important ideas should be placed before the group *simultaneously*: 1) consider other points of view, and 2) place aside actions that are incongruent with agreed upon objectives and goals. The idea is that you encourage expressing points of view without interjecting personal agendas.

Jean-Phillipe believed that an instrumental activity for the *Sleek Surface Maritime* development team was encouraging team members to express their concerns, doubts, and fears about the project. In most human endeavors that are aspirational, such as the goal of successfully implementing adaptations to minimize sea level rise, there is the possibility of failing. Jean-Phillipe felt encouraging team members to publicly voice their unspoken concerns, doubts, and fears bolstered a sense of interdependence and validated human emotions we all experience.

As the team facilitator, you have organized your notes from the conversation with Jean-Phillipe for presenting to your team this evening. You were asked by the team to include some insights from your past experiences. As you review the capabilities of Interdependent Thinking and Acting, you may consider: Which other practices listed under the three capabilities might propel the Nova Scotia Coastal Climate Collaborative team forward?

CAPABILITY: Establish and Maintain an Environment of Trust
Practices:

- Model the *predictable values* of integrity, transparency, and honesty
- Maintain a community with equal status and certainty in

ways of working together

- Model *predictable skills* (role competence) for working together
- Maintain an environment of psychological safety

CAPABILITY: Accept a Shared Understanding of Objectives, Approaches, and Challenges

Practices:

- Foster the acceptance and support of overarching coalition objectives and working group goals
- Create a shared understanding of challenges and agreed-upon approaches to addressing them
- Maintain continuous communication of common objectives and measures of success
- Develop the capacity to look at things from other points of view
- Place aside actions that are incongruent with agreed upon objectives and goals

CAPABILITY: Promote Access to Resources and Coordination Across a Broader Community

Practices:

- Establish opportunities for coalition partners to successfully share data, knowledge, expertise, and wisdom
- Establish practices for coalition partners to coordinate to avoid overlapping efforts and address overlooked activities
- Develop structures to share data, knowledge, resources, and insights of working groups (internal)
- Develop structures to share knowledge, resources, and insights with willing communities (external)

Appendix C
Adaptive Competence

BC Coastal Communities Climate Change Alliance

Port of Vancouver, British Columbia, and Steveston Harbour on the Fraser River and Nanaimo Harbour, on Vancouver Island, British Columbia

---

You invited today's presenter, Lincoln Angiak, on behalf of The BC Coastal Communities Climate Change Alliance, to share his knowledge and wisdom about adaptive competence during lunch. Two communities within your alliance are confronted with planning a managed retreat due to sea level rise. There are frameworks developed by other organizations that assist with the legal aspects of a managed retreat for communities. The BC Coastal Communities Climate Change Alliance team is especially interested in *how to prepare community leaders for the frontline work* of a managed retreat or adapting to the consequences of sea level rise.

Lincoln described his experiences as the skipper of the self-propelled barge *Kusko* delivering supplies and fuel to villages on the Kuskokwim River. Several of the fuel tank farms that Lincoln and the *Kusko* supplied with fuel are now being relocated due to severe riverbank erosion and thawing tundra. Villages are being relocated due to extreme weather events. He has been on the front line observing the disruption, stress, and anxiety that people experience when their way of life is in jeopardy. Lincoln emphasized that the people most impacted by the disruption need to feel that they have some control over any potential solutions and are equal partners in the process. He shared that partnerships can be challenging to form because of past trauma and poor treatment that have marginalized many Alaska Native people.

Lincoln suggested that some of the practices from Communicating to Understand and Influence and from Interdependent Acting and Thinking are critical to have in place *before* attempting to introduce the idea of adaptability. He said that a nominal level of trust must be established if any relationship between the BC Coastal Communities Climate Change Alliance and a community can be achieved. Lincoln emphasized that developing a trusting relationship takes patience and active listening when past events, present circumstances, and an uncertain future all intersect for individuals and communities.

Lincoln believes introducing the bridge view and the deck view is a critical practice for community leaders to understand. He shared that understanding the big picture and attending to even the smallest details is essential for assisting a community. Lincoln has observed that many big-picture plans can be drafted in the abstract. However, it is a local leader's knowledge and wisdom that informs *how* a bridge view/big picture plan impacts the lives of individual community members. Lincoln's final comment really resonated with you: "Plans almost always need adjustments, revisions, and adaptations when applied to real life circumstances."

As you organize your thoughts before presenting to the team, you wonder, what other Adaptive Competence practices might I share with my colleagues?

CAPABILITY: Understand and Analyze Complex Problems
Practices:

- Utilize current knowledge and apply it in a novel setting
- Develop the capacity to diagnose aspects of presenting problems
- Apply the *bridge* view and a *deck* view
- Understand and address technical problems and adaptive challenges

- Unbundle aspects of a problem while keeping the whole in mind
- Prioritize areas of focus and consider which areas might need attention first

CAPABILITY: Engage in Flexible Thinking to Address Complex Problems

Practices:

- Be willing to modify approaches based upon evidence
- Develop alternative strategies when adaptive challenges are encountered
- Model patience while designing potential solutions
- Communicate that problems are not intractable
- Seek and listen to diverse views

Endnotes

1 "1918-19: 'Spanish Influenza' Claims Millions of Lives," National Institute of Health, National Library of Medicine, accessed June 21, 2022, https://www.nlm.nih.gov/nativevoices/timeline/420.html.

2 Gary Whiteley, Lexie Domaradzki, Arthur Costa, Patty Muller, *Dispositions of Leadership: The Effects on Student Learning and School Culture* (Lanham, MD: Rowman & Littlefield, 2017), 41.

3 "The Water in You: Water and the Human Body," USGS, accessed May 22, 2019, https://usgs.gov/special-topics/water-science-school/science/water-you-water-and-human-body.

4 "Factsheet: People and Oceans," UN, June 2017, https://www.un.org/sustainabledevelopment/wp-content/uploads/2017/05/Ocean-fact-sheet-package.pdf.

5 Whiteley, et al., *Dispositions*, 47.

6 Whiteley, et al., *Dispositions*, 43.

7 Whiteley, et al., *Dispositions*, 42-43.

8 Ron Ritchhart, *Intellectual Character: What It Is, Why It Matters, and How We Get It* (San Francisco: Jossey-Bass, 2002), 31.

9 Whiteley, et al., *Dispositions*, 81.

10 Robert J. Garmston and Bruce M. Wellman, *The Adaptive School: A Sourcebook for Developing Collaborative Groups*, 3rd ed. (Lantham, MD: Rowman & Littlefield, 2016), 42–51.

11 Ibid., 41.

12 Ibid., 83–86.

13 Ibid., 60-61.

14 Ibid., 70.

15 Ibid., 58-59.

16 Whiteley, et al., *Dispositions*, 117.

17 Robert Reich, "Allocentric and Idiocentric Persuasion: Characteristics of Leadership Personality," March 2015, SSRN: https://ssrn.com/abstract=4024433.

18 "Arctic Circle Assembly," accessed October 15, 2022, https://www.arcticcircle.org/assemblies. The Arctic Circle Assembly meets annually in Reykjavik, Iceland. All organizations and individuals interested in addressing the unique challenges of the Arctic, and desiring to reach a global audience, are welcome to attend.

19 Ronald A. Heifetz, *Leadership Without Easy Answers* (Cambridge, MA: The Belknap Press of Harvard University Press, 1994), 107.

20 Ibid., 107.

21 "Vessel of Opportunity Program," SEAPRO, accessed September 20, 2021, https://www.seapro.org/voo.html.

22 "Big Data Analytics: What It Is and Why It Matters," SAS, accessed November 1, 2022, https://www.sas.com/en_us/insights/analytics/big-data-analytics.html#technical.

23 Catholic Online, World's Catholic Library home page, accessed November 1, 2022, https://www.catholic.org/saints/saint.php?-saint_id=209.

24 My Ship Tracking home page, accessed November 1, 2022, https:// www.myshiptracking.com/vessels/aotea-maersk-mmsi-2197910000-imo-9166778.

25 "The Lake of Port Revel," accessed August 20, 2020, https://www.portrevel.com/11063-the-lake-of-port-revel.htm.

26 Whiteley, et al., *Dispositions*, 112–114.

27 Arthur L. Costa and Robert J. Garmston, *Cognitive Coaching: Developing Self-Directed Leaders and Learners*, 3rd ed. (Lantham, MD: Rowman & Littlefield, 2016), 61.

28 Whiteley, et al., *Dispositions*, 117.

29 "Factsheet: American Indian/Alaska Native Veterans," Office of Health Equity Veterans Health Administration Department of Veterans Affairs, accessed August 21, 2022, https://www.va.gov/HEALTHEQUITY/docs/American_Indian_Heritage_Month_Fact_Sheet.pdf.

30 "Federal Agencies Could Enhance Support for Native Village Efforts to Address Environmental Threats," United States Government Accountability Office GAO-22-104241, May 18, 2022, https://www.gao.gov/products/gao-22-104241.

31 "Swinomish Climate Change Initiative Climate Adaptation Action Plan," Office of Planning and Community Development, Swinomish Indian Tribal Community, October 2010, https://www.swinomish-climate.com/swinomish-climate-change-initiative.

32 Robert Sternberg, "Adaptive Competence across Cultures and Subcultures," accessed November 1, 2022, www.robertjsternberg.com/new-page.

33 Kartina Bohle Carbonell, Renee Stalmeijer, Karen Konings, Mien Segers, Jeroen van Merrienboer, "How experts deal with novel situations: A review of adaptive expertise," *Educational Research Review*, no. 12, (2014): 14-29, https://doi.org/10.1016/j.edurev.2014.03.001.

34 Ronald Heifetz, Alexander Grashow, Marty Linsky, *The Practice of Adaptive Leadership: Tools and Tactics for Changing*

Your Organization and the World (Boston, MA: Harvard Business Press, 2009). 8. The authors popularized viewing situations from the balcony and the dance floor. It seemed prudent while aboard an ocean-going vessel to use the bridge view and the deck view. Mariners have used these vantage points since wooden ships sailed upon the open seas.

35 Ibid., 19-20.

36 Sharon Daloz Parks, Leadership Can Be Taught: A Bold Approach for a Complex World, (Boston, MA: Harvard Business School Publishing Corporation, 2005), 10.

37 Heifetz, et al., *Adaptive Leadership*, 16.

38 Barry Johnson, *Polarity Management: Identifying and Managing Unsolvable Problems* (Amherst, MA: HRD Press, 2014), xii-xix. Learning to apply polarity management requires learning a detailed process. Managing an ongoing dilemma, as used in the book, is a simpler idea that uses commonly understood vocabulary.

39 Whiteley, et al., *Dispositions*, 76–80.

Index

A

Adaptive Competence (disposition 2, day 5)
    about and definition of, xxv, 92*textbox2*, 93, 100*textbox3*
    for alternative strategies and modifications, 97–98
    bridge vs. deck views, 93*table15*, 94, 98–99, 98*table16*, 104, 109–110
    and climate action plans, 91–95, 101, 104
    complex problems and, 93–94*table15*, 95–96
    dim sum analogy, 100–101
    as a keystone disposition, 92–93, 100, 105
    in leadership, 99–103
    manageable dilemmas, 96–97, 101, 102*table17*, 104–105
    modeling patience and listening, 99
    technical vs. adaptive or identity issues, 94–97
    Worksheet for Examining and Initiative, 101, 102*table17*
agendas
    and effective meetings, 26–27, 28–29*table6*, 32
    personal/individual, 46
    and team member roles, 27*table5*
Alaska
    the CAGIS Team and, xxiii, 87–90, 89, 110, 113
    climate change in, ix–x, xiv, xx, 43, 125, 135
    Department of Education and Early Development, xix
    Quinhagak, xi, 87, 89, 90–91, 95
    State Department of Transportation, 110–111, 135
Alaska State Department of Transportation, 110–111
Alyeska Tug and Barge, 89, 90, 91
Angiak, Lincoln (CAGIS Team)
    background of, 87–92, 114
    as a fictional character, xi
    presentations of, 104, 106–111, 125–126
    and Traditional Ecological Knowledge (TEK), 67–68
    See also Adaptive Competence (disposition 2, day 5); CAGIS Team
Arctic Circle Assembly, 43

B
bridge vs. deck views, 93*table15*, 94, 98–99, 98*table16*, 104, 109–110

C
CAGIS Foundation
   about, xiv–xxv, xvi, 118
   Five-Day Leadership Training at Sea project, xxv–xxvi, 11–14
   See also CANAM Smart Ports and Harbors Program grant
CAGIS Team
   about the leaders, xxiii, xxiv–xxvi, 1, 4, 7–8, 57
   facilitator role, 20–21, 27*table5*, 29, 31, 65, 119–120, 123
   the Five-Day Leadership Training at Sea project, xxv–xxvi
   listener role, 14, 82, 84*table14*
   in meetings, 27*table5*
   predictable skills (role competence) and, 44, 46–47, 124
   process observer role, 27*table5*, 29, 32
   recorder and disseminator role, 27*table5*, 29
   See also Angiak, Lincoln; Gagnon, Jean-Philippe; Hansen, Marit-Abril; Jensen, Nora; Knudsen, Erika
CAGIS Team debrief
   deck vs. bridge views, 93*table15*, 94, 98–99, 98*table16*, 104, 109–110
   dialogue about, 108–109
   external grant evaluators, 110–111
   as Gathering Information for Improvement and Innovation exercise, 109–110
   informal, 106–107
   Lincoln Angiak's reflections, 110–111
   Marit-Abril Hansen's reflections, 111–116
   purpose of, 108
California Maritime Academy (Cal Maritime), 14–15
CANAM Norms
   critical practices and definition of, 22–23, 23–24*table3*
   for discussion and dialogue, 99
   elements of an effective meeting, 28–29*table6*, 32, 34, 47, 65, 80
   for productive team collaboration, 22–26, 35, 47, 67–68, 80*table13* 96, 99
   for trust, 96
   See also discussion and dialogue; listening; modeling; trust; working agreements
CANAM Smart Ports and Harbors Program grant
   about, goals and objectives, xi, xiii, xxiv–xxv, 43, 58

building capacity, 22, 48–49, 49, 52, 93
building leadership frameworks, 12–13, 15–16, 22, 56, 100, 109
case studies, xvi, 48, 49–50, 52
creating useable case studies, xvi, 48, 49–50, 52
developing community frameworks, 48, 49, 50–51, 115, 125
equipment, 66
Five-Day Leadership Training at Sea, xxv–xxvi
information gathering and monitoring equipment, 66
itinerary and schedule, 6–8
mission, 12*textbox1*, 48, 64, 103, 108
program establishment and coastal zones, 1–4
"shakedown cruise" simulation, 4–5
See also dispositions of leadership

CANAM Team protocols
Descriptive Feedback Protocol, 74, 78, 80–82, 82–84*table14*, 120, 123
for discussion and dialogue, 18, 63–65, 82–84*table14*, 120, 123
feedback for adult learning and growth, 83*table13*, 84
for structuring conversations, 82–83, 84*table14*
See also paraphrasing; processes and protocols

capabilities and practices
of Adaptive Competence, 100, 104–105
for all dispositions, xxvi–xxvii, 3, 13
for Communicating to Understand and Influence, 16, 38, 40
establishing and maintaining an environment of trust, 44*table8*, 45–47
for Gathering Information for Improvement and Innovation, 65–68
group competencies and, 30, 34–35
and the "how" of practice, 8
for Interdependent Thinking and Acting, 43, 44–45*table8*
and leadership as a *contingency activity*, xv
modes of intelligence and, xv, 12
for Seeking Support and Feedback that Fosters Growth, 75–76*table12*, 76–79
of self-awareness and self-knowledge, 19, 74–78, 75*table12*, 85, 112
shared understanding and, 44*table8*, 48–51
teaching of, 13
trust and, 44*table8*, 45–47
See also CANAM Norms; dispositions of leadership; modeling

case studies, xvi, 48, 49–50, 52
Center for Evaluation, Policy, and Research (CEPR) (Indiana University), 110, 111

characters (team leaders). *See* CAGIS Team leaders
clarity, 29, 31, 39, 46, 83
climate change
   in Alaska/the Arctic, ix–x, xiv, xx, 43, 125, 135
   BC Coastal Communities Climate Change Alliance and, 105, 125–127
   community adaptation to, 17, 50, 113–114, 116
   decision-making processes and, 64, 67
   green hydrogen power, 42, 90
   impacts on communities and, 111, 118, 135
   leadership and, xiii–xiv, xiii–xvi, xvi–xvii, xxvii
   Nova Scotia Coast Climate Collaborative, 122–123
   rising sea levels and, 17
   Swinomish Climate Change Initiative Climate Adaptation Action Plan, 91, 92, 101–102
   and village migrations/relocations, ix–x, 90
climigration, xiii
coastal communities, xxv, 50–51
   See also climate change; engaging communities; Indigenous Peoples and communities
coastal zones
   about/itinerary, 6–8
   Port of Halifax, 2, 50, 55, 62, 66, 122–124
   Port of Pascagoula, 2, 40, 50, 66, 119–121
   Port of Vancouver, 2, 5*map*, 6–8, 15, 50, 62, 66, 105, 125–127
Coast Guard, 2, 42, 88–89
collaboration and cooperation
   CANAM Norms for, 22–26, 35, 47, 67–68, 80*table13*, 96, 99
   vs. competition, 77–78, 77–78
   leadership styles and, xiii–xvi
   seven topics, 80*table13*
   and trust, xvii, 106
   See also equal status; trust; trust-building
Communicating to Understand and Influence (disposition 1, day 1)
   about, xxv, 6–7
   capabilities and practices for, 16, 38, 40
   for Cultivating Productive Working Relationships, 17, 18*table1*, 21–24, 43, 120
   for Developing Personal Presence, 17, 18*table1*, 19–21, 120
   discussion and dialogue, 29–31
   feedback and team performance, 32–33

inclusion and diversity, 33–38, 36–37*table7*
sequencing, 38
working agreements and agendas for, 25–29, 120
community engagement. *See* engaging communities
Compute Canada, 62
contingency activity, xv
critical practices, 22–24

D
data
    decision-making and, 49, 50, 59*table9*, 60–61, 62*table10*, 109–110
    gathering, 58, 58*table9*, 60–61, 69, 110
    quantitative and qualitative, 58, 58*table9*, 60–61, 69, 110
    sharing, 62–63, 63*table11*
Data Carpentry, 62
Deadliest Catch, The (television program), 38
decision-making
    authority vs. dialogue, 29–30, 39–40, 99
    and community information gathering and engagement and, 64, 66, 97
    ethical vs. self-interest, xv–xvi
    and evidence-based data gathering, 49, 50, 59*table9*, 60–61, 62*table10*, 109–110
deck vs. bridge views, 93*table15*, 94, 98, 98–99, 98*table16*, 104, 109–110
Deepwater Horizon oil spill, xvi
Descriptive Feedback Protocol, 74, 78, 80–82, 82–84*table14*, 120, 123
discussion and dialogue
    clarity and, 29, 31, 39, 46, 83
    vs. decision-making, 29–31, 39–40, 65
    discussion vs. dialogue, 29–31, 39–40, 65, 99
    for feedback and support, 76*table11*, 80–84
    to identify common interests and concerns, x, 8
    identifying common concerns, x, 8
    protocols and processes for, 18, 63–65, 82–84*table14*, 120, 123
    in the team debriefing, 107–108, 111
    See also Communicating to Understand and Influence (disposition 1, day 1);
        equal status; listening; paraphrasing; Questions to Engage Your Thinking
disposition 1. *See* Communicating to Understand and Influence (disposition 1, day 1)
disposition 2. *See* Adaptive Competence (disposition 2, day 5)
disposition 3. *See* Gathering Information for Improvement and Innovation
    (disposition 3, day 3)

disposition 4. *See* Interdependent Thinking and Acting (disposition 4, day 2)
disposition 5. *See* Seeking Support and Feedback that Fosters Growth (disposition 5, day 4)
dispositions of leadership
  about, xv, xxiv–xxvii, 16, textbox2
  and *group effectiveness*, 79, 119
  See also specific dispositions
Dispositions of Leadership: The Effects on Student Learning and School Culture, xix
diversity
  and predictable skills, 47
  reasons for and benefits of, 33–34, 38
  strategies for supporting, 36–37*table7*, 80*table13*

E
empathy, x, xvi, 14, 18, 36, 120
empathy fatigue, 78
engaging communities
  and adaptive competence, 45*table7*, 50–52
  as a capability and practice, 48–49, 51–52
  and information gathering, 63–64, 66, 69–70, 97
  Traditional Ecological Knowledge (TEK) and, xv, 50, 66–67, 91, 92
equal status
  and collaborative decision-making, xv, xvi, 33, 67–68
  interpersonal communication and, 22–23, 30–31, 125
  for productive working relationships, 36, 44, 67, 96, 123–124
Erika. *See* Knudsen, Erika

F
Five-Day Leadership Training at Sea project, xxv–xxvi, 11–14
five dispositions. *See* dispositions of leadership

G
Gagnon, Jean-Philippe (CAGIS Team)
  background, xxiii, 14, 41–43, 54, 73, 78, 89–90, 98
  on the Nova Scotia Coast Climate Collaborative, 122–123
  reflections on the voyage, 106, 115, 118
  See also CAGIS Team; Interdependent Thinking and Acting (disposition 4, day 2)
Gathering Information for Improvement and Innovation (disposition 3, day 3)

about, xxv, 57–58
data sharing, 62–63, 63*table11*
for decision-making, 59*table9*, 61–62*table10*, 65–66
discussion protocols and dialogue processes, 64–65
open-mindedness for improvement, 59–60*table8*, 67–68
with openness and transparency, 63–64
quantitative and qualitative data, 58, 58*table9*, 60–61, 69, 110
seeking multiple perspectives and points of view, 66–67
great man leadership style (leader-centric), vs. collaborative, xiii
green hydrogen, 42, 90
Grimsson, Ólafur Ragnar, 43
group effectiveness, 79, 119
group identity, 3–4, 8, 30–31, 33, 41, 96, 108
Gulf Coast Sea Level Rise Consortium, 40, 119

H

Hansen, Marit-Abril (CAGIS Team), 3–4, 14–15, 43, 64, 64–65, 79, 89, 106–114, 116–119
background, xxiii, 14–15, 89
collegiality of, 43, 78
demeanor, xi
influence on the voyage, 3–4, 79
on process vs. authority, 39–40
reflections on the voyage, 106–114, 116–119
See also CAGIS Team; Communicating to Understand and Influence (disposition 1, day 1)
home group teams, 15, 24, 25, 79
honesty
humility and integrity, 74
integrity and transparency, 44, 46, 55, 96, 109, 123
and trust, 44–46, 53, 55, 96, 123
humility, 74, 76–77, 85

I

identity
adaptive problem-solving and, 94–97
group, 3–4, 8, 30–31, 33, 41, 96, 108
indigenous Peoples and communities
impact of climate change on, 111, 118, 125

and Sainte-Foy Marine, Ltd., 73
Swinomish Indian Tribe, 91, 91–92, 101
Traditional Ecological Knowledge (TEK), xv, 50, 66–67, 91, 92
integrity
    honesty and transparency, 44, 46, 55, 74, 96, 109, 123
    and moral purpose, 113–114, 116
    trust, 44–46, 53, 55, 96, 123
intelligence or modes of thinking, xv, 12
Interdependent Thinking and Acting (disposition 4, day 2)
    about, xxv, 43–44
    capabilities overview, 43, 44–45*table8*
    case studies, xvi, 48, 49–50, 52
    coordination and synchrony, 43
    knowledge sharing structures, 52–53
    resource access and coordination, 45*table7*, 51–52
    and shared understanding, 44–45*table8*, 48–51
    and trust, 44*table8*, 45–47, 96
    See also trust; trust-building

J

Jean-Philippe. *See* Gagnon, Jean-Philippe
Jensen, Nora (CAGIS Team), 67, 71–73, 85–86, 106–111, 114
    See also CAGIS Team; Seeking Support and Feedback that Fosters Growth (disposition 5, day 4)

K

Knudsen, Erika (CAGIS Team), 56–57, 69, 72, 78, 92, 106–111, 114, 116
    See also Gathering Information for Improvement and Innovation (disposition 3, day 3)
Kuskokwim
    Lower Kuskokwin School District, ix–xi, xx
    river system and bay, 87–88, 89, 110, 125

L

leadership
    climate change and, xiii–xiv, xiii–xvi, xvi–xvii, xxvii
    as a *contingency activity*, xv
    as demonstrating capabilities and practices, xv
    forms of intelligence, xv, 12

interpersonal vs. intrapersonal aspects of, 73
modeling positivity, 18, 20–21, 36, 120
and self-awareness, 74–77, 85, 112
styles, xiii
See also CANAM Norms; collaboration and cooperation; discussion and dialogue; dispositions of leadership; integrity; listening; modeling; self-awareness and self-knowledge; trust; trust-building

Lincoln. *See* Angiak, Lincoln
listeners (team role), 14, 82, 84*table14*
listening
and the Descriptive Feedback Protocol, 80–82, 82–84*table14*
to develop trust, 126
and equal status, 67–68, 96
paraphrasing, x, 13, 18–20, 23, 27, 36, 81–82, 82*table14*, 84, 99, 120
and personal presence, x, 18*table1*, 19, 36*table7*, 120
positivity vs. negativity and, 20–21
to support diversity, 89, 94, 99, 101, 127
to understand, xvi, 13–14, 22, 23*table3*, 36, 39
See also Descriptive Feedback Protocol; paraphrasing

Lopez, Barry, xiii–xiv, xviii

M

Maersk (shipping company), 72–73
Marit-Abril. *See* Hansen, Marit-Abril
meetings
agendas, 26–27
elements of effectiveness, 28–29*table6*, 32
team member roles, 27*table5*
memoranda of understanding (MOUs), 63
mentoring
in maritime industries, 42, 80, 89, 112
and professional development, 14, 84, 114, 117
in school administrations, xix–xx, 135
SEAfarers Mentoring Model (SEE), 73–74, 78
migrations and relocations
of animals, 49, 66
climigration, xiii
of people, ix–x, 90
modeling

CAGIS norms and protocols, 74, 106, 116
and the Descriptive Feedback Protocol, 74
flexibility, 7, 51, 93, 97
integrity, transparency and honesty, 44, 46, 123
patience, 94, 99, 127
positivity, 18, 20–21, 36, 120
role competence, 44, 124

N
Nora. *See* Jensen, Nora
Nova Scotia Coastal Climate Collaborative, 122–123

O
openness
    and competence, 47
    and transparency, 22, 24*table3*, 36*table7*, 59*table8*, 63–64, 67

P
paraphrasing
    to demonstrate understanding, 18–20, 23, 36*table7*, 99, 120
    and integrating practices and skills, 13, 27, 82*table14*, 84*table14*
    for productive community dialogue, x, 81–82
Port of Halifax coastal zone, 2, 50, 55, 62, 66, 122–124
Port of Pascagoula coastal zone, 2, 40, 50, 66, 119–121
Port of Vancouver coastal zone, 2, 5*map*, 7, 8, 50, 62, 66, 105, 125–127
predictable skills (role competence), 44, 46–47, 124
predictable values (integrity, transparency and honesty), 44–46, 55, 96, 123
problem-solving
    and reflection, x–xi, 29, 104–105
    technical vs. identity (emotional) aspects of, 94–97
    See also decision-making; discussion and dialogue
processes and protocols
    for decision-making, 39–40, 64–65, 67
    for discussion and dialogue, 18, 63–65, 82–84*table14*, 120, 123
    the process observer's role, 27*table5*, 29, 32
    See also CANAM Norms; CANAM Team Protocols; samples; working agreements

Q

quantitative and qualitative data, 58, 58*table9*, 60–61, 69, 110
Questions to Engage Your Thinking
   about Adaptive Competence, 104–105
   about collaboration, 9–10
   about Communicating to Understand and Influence, 39–40
   about the debrief, 117–118
   about Developing Interdependent Thinking and Acting, 54–55
   about Gathering Information for Improvement and Innovation, 69–70
   about leadership and environmental challenges, xxvii
   about Seeking Support and Feedback, 85–86
   about training and the Wheelhouse simulation, 9–10
Quinhagak, Alaska, xi, 87, 89, 90–91, 95

R

race, nationality and ethnicity, xiii, 56–57, 72
reflections
   group effectiveness and, 27, 75, 119
   for improvement and innovation, 108, 111–112, 113, 115
   and problem-solving and learning, x–xi, 29, 104–105
relational trust, 38, 40, 52
Respectful & Productive Relationships program (Knudsen), 57, 72, 74
role competence (predictable skills). *See* trust-building
RV Smart Ports
   about, xxiii, 4, 11
   planning for the voyage, 6–8
   and the Vancouver Harbour coastal zone, 15

S

Sainte-Foy Marine, Ltd., 4, 14, 42, 47, 54, 73, 78, 89, 91
St. Walburga (barge), 71–72
salmon fishing, 38, 56, 87–88, 89
samples
   comment pattern for developing personal presence, 20–21*table2*
   and meeting roles, 27*table5*
   for personal presence, 20–21*table2*
   of working agreements, 26*table4*, 63, 80
   worksheets, 25, 101–102
scientific knowledge vs. Traditional Ecological Knowledge (TEK), xv

SEAfarers Mentoring Model (SEE), 73–74, 78
sea levels, 17
Seeking Support and Feedback that Fosters Growth (disposition 5, day 4)
    about, xxv, 74–75
    CANAM Team Protocols, 82–84
    collegial dialogue and constructive feedback, 80–82
    professional system for, 75–76*table12*, 78–79
    self-knowledge and self-awareness and, 75*table12*, 76–79
self-awareness and self-knowledge, 19, 74–78, 75*table12*, 85, 112
self-confidence, 85
self-discipline, 81
self-interest, xv, xvii
Sleek Surface Maritime, 41, 42
Swinomish Climate Change Initiative Climate Adaptation Action Plan, 91, 92, 101
Swinomish Indian Tribe, 91, 91–92, 101

T
Traditional Ecological Knowledge (TEK), xv, 50, 66–67, 91, 92
transparency
    and fairness, 30
    honesty and integrity, 44–46, 55, 96, 109, 123
    openness and, 22, 24*table3*, 36*table7*, 59*table8*, 63–64, 67
    trust, 44–46, 53, 55, 96, 123
trust
    and collaboration, xvii, 106
    and Communicating to Understand and Influence, 40
    creating an environment of, 43–47, 44*table8*, 109
    and interdependence, 52–54, 122–124, 126
    relational, 38, 40, 52
trust-building
    as condition of effective coordination to reach objectives, 43
    predictable skills (role competence) and, 44, 46–47, 124
    predictable values of (integrity, transparency and honesty), 44–46, 55, 96, 123

V
vessel of opportunity (VOO) programs, 49, 65–66
vessels
    Abril Mia, 113

green hydrogen powered container ships, 42, 90
Katmai, 89
Kusko (tugboat), 89, 91, 95, 125
Nordic Quest, 89, 95
Nordic Dreki, 113
USCGC *Alex Haley*, 88

W
wisdom keepers, xiii
women and gender, 37, 71–73, 112
working agreements
    for Communicating to Understand and Influence, 18, 24, 25–29, 34, 36*table7*, 120
    cooperation agreements, 2
    for Gathering Information for Improvement and Innovation, 63
    for Interdependent Thinking and Acting, 44, 47
    samples, 26*table4*, 63, 80
    for Seeking Support and Feedback to Foster Growth, 80
    See also processes and protocols; samples

Y
Yup'ik people and culture, 87–90

About the Author

Gary Whiteley has been a medical laboratory technician, truck driver, residential home builder, painter, commercial fisher, university residence hall director, and hockey coach. Gary has also been an educator for forty-two years. He served in roles at the school level and district level, including classroom teacher, assistant principal, school principal, and assistant superintendent. Gary earned a doctorate in educational leadership at the University of Maine. He developed and facilitated mentoring programs that served school principals and superintendents for the Alaska Department of Education and Early Development. Gary designed and implemented two statewide leadership programs in Idaho for school principals. He was a leadership consultant for the Education Commission of the States for five years. Gary resides in Alaska—the Great Land—where the impact of global climate change is unavoidable.

www.ingramcontent.com/pod-product-compliance
Lightning Source LLC
LaVergne TN
LVHW041947070526
838199LV00051BA/2929